Contents

Criminal Prosperity

About MOST

MOST (www.unesco.org/most) is a research programme designed by UNESCO to promote international comparative social science research. Its primary emphasis is to support large-scale, long-term autonomous research and to disseminate the relevant findings and data to decision-makers. The programme operates in three priority research areas:

1 the management of change in multi-cultural and multi-ethnic societies
2 cities and arenas experiencing accelerated social transformation
3 local and regional strategies for coping with economic, technological and environmental change.

About the author

Guilhem Fabre is a sinologist and socio-economist, and a professor at the Faculté des Affaires Internationales at the University of Le Havre (France). His most recent publication is: *Le miroir chinois de la transition*, L'Harmattan, Paris, 2001.

Criminal Prosperity

Drug Trafficking, Money Laundering and
Financial Crises after the Cold War

Guilhem Fabre

Scientific coordinator for the Asian network
of UNESCO's MOST Drugs Project

Taylor & Francis Group

LONDON AND NEW YORK

First published in French in 1999
under the title *Les Prospérites du Crime*
by Éditions de l'Aube

Revised and first published in English in 2003
by RoutledgeCurzon
11 New Fetter Lane, London EC4P 4EE

Simultaneously published in the USA and Canada
by RoutledgeCurzon
29 West 35th Street, New York, NY 10001

RoutledgeCurzon is an imprint of the Taylor & Francis Group

© 2003 Guilhem Fabre

Typeset in Stempel Garamond by LaserScript Ltd, Mitcham, Surrey
Printed and bound in Great Britain by
MPG Books Ltd, Bodmin

British Library Cataloguing in Publication Data
A catalogue record of this book is available from the British Library

Library of Congress Cataloging in Publication Data
A catalog record for this book has been requested

ISBN 0–7007–1498–7

This book was published with the financial assistance of the
Management of Social Transformations (MOST) Programme of UNESCO

The ideas and opinions expressed in this publication are those of the author
and do not necessarily represent the views of UNESCO. The designations
employed and the presentation of material throughout the publication do
not imply the expression of any opinion whatsoever on the part of
UNESCO concerning the legal status of any country, territory, city or area
or of its authorities, or concerning its frontiers or boundaries.

Introduction

———◆———

Since the end of the Cold War, there has been a worldwide increase in corruption, organized crime, drug trafficking and drug consumption. This book sets out to define the relations between these three phenomena: first with an historic statement of their convergence in the nineteenth century, then by looking at the current extent of the illicit economy. At the end of the twentieth century the UN and the International Monetary Fund estimate the turnover of organized crime at US$1000 billion, in other words 3 per cent of the world gross domestic product. Approximately one half of this figure is connected to drug trafficking, the most notorious area of crime. Research shows that there is no criminal network which specializes solely in drugs. Organized crime takes advantage of a group of illicit activities: smuggling, dealing in arms and fissile materials, dealing in and procuring labour, the export of dangerous and toxic objects, dealing in stolen vehicles, in archaeological artefacts and objects of art, etc. In addition, it can be seen that these multiple service networks are supported by the globalization of trade.

An historical perspective, contemplated in the first chapter through the example of the Middle Empire and more generally of Asia, provides a picture of incestuous links that have been forged between opium, colonial expansion and corruption. The end of the Cold War corresponds to a worldwide expansion of the market economy comparable to the situation which prevailed before the war of 1914–18. This movement marks the renewal of an illicit economy, of drug trafficking and corruption in emergent countries and those in transition. The example of China, developed in Chapter 2, allows us to analyse the institutional, social and geopolitical stakes related to the reappearance of drugs in a country where they were practically eliminated after the revolution of 1949.

The economic effects of drug trafficking, and in a larger sense of organized crime, are taken into consideration in Chapter 3, where the question of laundering is first considered. One of the essential paradoxes of policies against drugs is that criminalization has tended to focus on drug consumption while the laundering of profits, which constitutes the central activity for the economic market, remains practically unpunished. Despite the calls made for the decriminalization of consumption by many practitioners and by the ex-General Secretary of Interpol, Raymond Kendall, prisons have been filled with user–sellers who feed the cycle for the future. In the United States, for example, two-thirds of the 2 million people detained in prison have serious drug problems.

In contrast to drug consumption, which is kept constantly in the public eye, the laundering of drug profits goes on in relative obscurity. Even though court cases regularly throw light on the involvement of prominent figures, including some heads of state, public opinion remains confused about the qualitative leap which has been made by organized crime. Not very long ago, one of the most lucrative crimes was bank robbery, whereas the great breach of law now consists in depositing money in the bank. The main threat is no longer the robber but the banker, whose co-operation must often be bought so that suspicious transactions are not disclosed. In other words, *corruption is becoming* the *crime weapon*. The banking profession, with its social prestige, has an image of integrity that keeps it fairly safe from the temptations to which it may be exposed. And since public opinion is amply supplied with anecdotes about various mafias, it harbours few suspicions about bankers. However, the very high yields of globalized financial markets have accustomed numerous operators to profit margins that cannot be obtained in real production, but are easy to negotiate in laundering activities, which pay between 25–30 per cent on investments.

The convergence among the licit, illicit and criminal spheres is facilitated by hypertrophied financing and by the guaranteed confidentiality of many offshore centres. The effects of this convergence, analysed in very general terms by the IMF, are already considerable. As the following pages show, there are links between money laundering and financial destabilization in the crises undergone by Mexico (Chapter 5), Thailand (Chapter 6) and Japan (Chapter 4), and that finally spread to all of Asia and indeed the world. If the strongest allies of organized crime are fear and silence, it is time to cast light on crime's prosperity, which is the great motive for its economic and political expansion.

1

The Mirror of History

——◆——

At the start of the 1990s, the report of the Financial Action Task Force formed by the Arche Summit estimated a net income of US$85 billion from drug trafficking in the United States and in Europe.[1] The scope of these funds, equivalent to half of the world's direct foreign investments or twice the turnover of the arms trade[2] in the same period, illustrates the increasing influence of drugs revenue on the international economy and on politics.

The fall of the communist regimes and the unification of capitalism around a neo-liberal creed, have since opened new horizons for the production of drugs, which has increased and diversified trafficking, which has become globalized due to contacts made between criminal organizations in all regions of the world. In the meantime, drug consumption has grown in rich countries and the number of drug producers and forwarding agents has increased considerably in Third World countries. Corruption is being trivialized and the penetration of the Mafia within the State apparatus is becoming increasingly important.

With the increase in trafficking, 70 to 90 per cent of which is comprised of the cocaine and heroin trade in industrialized countries,[3] the gap between legality and reality continues to grow. If the prohibition of drugs, reaffirmed by the Vienna

1

Convention in 1988, continues to be a general rule, the diversity of national laws and their application can sometimes be unharmonious; as, for example, within the European Union, where Italy tolerates the consumption of 0.3 grams of heroin per day, the Netherlands 0.5 grams, while France still theoretically continues to penalize the consumption of soft drugs.[4]

The question of prohibition or of de-penalizing refers to the possibility of establishing a world law on drugs, reconciling, in the framework of a common law, the interests of producing, transit and consumer countries. However, nothing seems to be more remote judging from past experiences and actual realities: drugs have always been a high value-added product, capable of modifying the terms of trade between countries and facilitating the rapid accumulation of capital. The weight of this economic logic is rendered just as well by history as by the international dynamics of the post-Cold War period, as we will analyse through the example of China.

Opium and colonization

The expansion of drug production, trafficking and of consumption has been closely related to western expansionism in Asia. When the English decided to colonize the Indies, with the nomination of Governor General Warren Hastings, they were the first, as of 1773, to use the monopoly of the opium production that they had inherited from the Moguls and from the Dutch, as a source of fiscal revenues. At this time, opium exports, principally to China, provided approximately one-seventh of the total revenue of the British Indies.[5]

Originally introduced to China as a medicine by Arab merchants during the Tang Dynasty (seventh–ninth centuries), tobacco mixed with opium was only used as of the 1720s. Despite a primary decree by the Emperor Yongzheng in 1729 forbidding the import of opium for non-medicinal purposes and ordering that opium den managers be executed (by means of strangulation), opium use became widespread, as explained by Jonathan Spence, among the richer classes, or in certain diverse social groups: the eunuchs of the Court, official Manchus, rich women who lacked education and who were confined in their houses, auxiliary civil servants, merchants and students preparing for or passing exams. In the 1770s, Charles de Constant observed that the Chinese had developed 'a passion for this narcotic which surpasses all beliefs'.[6] Later, in the nineteenth century, the smoking habit became increasingly popular among the coolies who consumed a local opium of much lower quality but which was more accessible. Certain employers who noticed the physical performances obtained under the effects of the drug, would even put opium at the disposal of workers.[7] Opium and its by-products, such as laudanum, already consumed in the West, were also seen as a true panacea in times when medical skills were still rudimentary. These products were used for pain control, malaria and chronic dysentery, which affected the Chinese population. They were even used to fight cholera.[8]

After having established its monopoly of opium collection, the British East India Company sold commercial licences to certain registered negotiators, in order to avoid being directly implicated in an illegal activity in China: theoretically the ships engaged in trafficking would have been confiscated.[9] Governor General Warren Hastings deplored the imbalance of trade in Sino–British commerce, which was reduced to the port of Canton and monopolized by the guild of the Cohong merchants. The Manchu Empire had accumulated trade surpluses by its exports of high value products – porcelain, tea, silk – which were not compensated by the demand for cotton, wool, fur, jewellery or English pewter. One reason for the prosperity during the reign of Qianlong (1736–1796) was the surplus of silver metal. This paid for the British purchases and injected energy into the economy of the southern provinces. These surpluses went from 3 million teals in the 1760s up to 7.5 million in the 1770s, then increased again to 16 million in the 1780s.[10]

To cope with this situation of commercial imbalance, Indian opium began to be conceived as trade money. This 'pernicious luxury article', according to Warren Hastings, 'which should not have been authorised unless for foreign trade',[11] allowed a limit to be placed on the metal-silver distribution since opium sales were allocated to the purchase of articles that the English provided in China. It is interesting to reveal that these results were obtained in the context of prohibition reinforcement. In 1800, an imperial decree forbade both the importation and the local production of opium. Commanders of foreign ships who consented to smuggling were liable for prosecution and imprisonment. In 1813, another decree forbade civil servants from consuming opium, with the punishment, if caught, of receiving 100 bamboo lashes and being displayed in public for two months wearing a *cangue*, a large piece of wood into which the head and hands were inserted. These measures had no effect on the trafficking, since it was organized around pirate groups or secret societies, with the complicity of corrupt officials. The ships which had opium on board were discharged into 'storage-ships' anchored near the island of Lintin, between Canton and Hong Kong, and their cargo was then distributed to junks, serving the coasts of Guangdong and Fujian. The expansion of trafficking mainly resulted from a planned increase in opium supply from Bengal and from the control taken by the English of the roads and of the harbours of opium transits in Malwa. Opium was cultivated in the central and North-western states of India which did not fall under their jurisdiction.[12] In 1824, the British East India Company extended its monopoly to an entire opium harvest in Malwa, but this policy did not overcome the competition from private merchants in Malwa, the export into China including opium which went through Bengal until the end of the 1820s.[13] Between 1790 and 1838, opium sales in China greatly increased (Table 1.1).

Following a stable period during the Napoleonic Wars, trafficking increased due to a number of factors. The

Table 1.1 British opium trade in China 1729–1900

Year	Number of cases	Tonnage
1729	200	14
1750	600	42
1773	1,000	70
1790	4,054	283
1800	4,570	320
1810	4,968	347
1816	5,106	357
1823	7,082	495
1828	13,131	919
1832	23,570	1649
1835	30,000	2100
1838	40,000	2800
1865	76,000	5320
1884	81,000	5670
1900	50,000	3500

Source: Jonathan Spence: *The Search for Modern China, Chinese Roundabout, Essays in Chinese History and Culture.* The average weight of one case is estimated here at 70 kg (Cf. Chantal Descours-Gatin, note 8, p. 7).

prohibition reinforcement in China forced the East India Company to stop accrediting certain merchants for opium commerce, and to sell its monopolized production to auctioneers. The abundance of both supply and competition was the result of an increasing number of merchants and adventurers, who were attracted by the opportunities for profit. This, however, decreased the sale price of Indian opium in China. Its consumption thus spread to the lower classes, who were satisfied even if the local opium was of a poorer quality. As of the 1820s, opium purchases represented *half of Chinese imports*[14] and satisfied one million smokers.[15] In 1831, a report by the great secretary of the Qing Court revealed that 'among the governor generals and their subordinates, at all military and civil levels of the hierarchy, those who *do not smoke* opium are very few'.[16] Despite an arsenal of prohibitionist reinforcement in 1831, the fall of the East India Company's monopoly on the Anglo-Saxon trade in 1834 did little more than increase Chinese drug imports, in that it encouraged the direct presence of British merchants in Canton, the number of which increased from 66 to 106, in only three years.[17] From 1829 to 1839, the annual opium imports coming from India reached an average of 1841 tons, in other words six times more than the average between 1811 and 1821.[18] These massive Chinese purchases led to a reversal of the balance of trade at China's expense, especially in the Southern provinces. The increasing scarcity of means of payment reduced the trade by depressing the prices of agricultural products and depressing growth. Whereas in the 1820s, two million taels left China each year, in the 1830s, this average reached more than 9 million.[19]

Faced with these difficulties, the Emperor Daoguang (1821–1850) re-launched the debate on the efficiency of the prohibition policy. In 1836, the partisans in favour of a re-organization law, grouped around the Vice-Minister of Ceremonies, emphasized the negative consequences of prohibition on general commerce. They proposed maintaining the smoking prohibition for civil servants, soldiers and the intellectual classes, by developing a new framework for drug importation. Thus, opium would be accepted as a medicine, would bear a customs duty, and its business would remain under the monopoly of Chinese traders, limited to barter. This measure aimed to limit drug consumption, to augment fiscal resources, to halt the loss of silver-money, to reduce the corruption of civil servants and to stimulate the production of local opium, which would, in the long run, become a substitute for Indian opium. The support of the Cantonese authorities for these proposals, however, re-launched a levy protest of the prohibitionist clan in Peking: the president of the council of rituals and the deputy head of the military department raised the issue of moral degradation and the social dangers related to the drug. They saw a need to reinforce repressive legislation and to punish foreign and Chinese traffickers equally.

This debate gave the general impression that the opium commerce was going to be legalized in Canton. The English put all their resources into augmenting poppy farming in India and increasing supplies.[20] But the Emperor Daoguang was finally in favour of reinforcing prohibition, sending his Commissioner Lin Zexu to Canton who, upon his arrival in May 1839, took strong measures: people who smoked were arrested, their pipes were confiscated and, after a blockade of six weeks, 20 000 drug cases held by foreign merchants were confiscated and destroyed, launching the Opium War.

William Jardine, the merchant who made a fortune in the drug trafficking business with his associate James Matheson, thanks to a great fleet of five brigs, seven schooners and nine navy depots scattered between Hong Kong and the Chinese coasts, played an important role in this conflict. Upon his return to London in 1839, this opium merchant knew how to obtain support from a manufacturing and textile lobby group to denounce the restriction that limited his commercial rights. On 27 September 1839, during a hearing granted by Prime Minister Palmerston, William Jardine exposed, with the support of maps, a campaign plan giving details of necessary arms, strengths and ships.[21] An expedition corps armed with gunboats was despatched, despite the moral objections of the missions and the indignation of Gladstone in the House of Commons, and after two years of quarrels and conflict, the opium traffic was freed. Article 4 of the Treaty of Nanking signed in 1842, imposed at the Manchu Court compensation of 6 million silver Mexican dollars for 'opium delivered in Canton'. No other disposition took place concerning the drug in this agreement that put the first Opium War to an end. However opium smuggling continued in the five harbours initially open to British merchants, then French and American, up until the legalization of importation 'for medical reasons' following the second Opium War in 1858. Following Hong Kong, which specialized in the transit of the drug from the moment the Treaty of Nanking was signed, Shanghai established itself as the centre for this tolerated traffic: the city imported more than 20 000 cases of opium (1400 t.) at the end of the

1840s and more than 30 000 cases (2100 t.) at the end of the 1850s.

Between 1850 and 1870, foreign merchants increasingly used opium as a bargaining tool in the purchase of Chinese products. To bypass the legislation which restrained commerce in certain harbours, in 1855 David Jardine and Donald Matheson, successors of their respective uncles, sent their Chinese agent, compradore Ahee, to Suzhou with a cargo of 440 000 dollars' worth of spices and opium to negotiate for the exchange of silk and tea. The use of opium as a means of payment became very common in domestic business.[22] During the same period, two decades of interior rebellions confronted the Manchu Empire requiring substantial financial resources to re-establish order. The conflicts, related to the Taipings revolt, resulted in more than 30 million victims and devastated the lower valley of the Yangtze. The provincial governments allowed the development of poppy farming, which was able to cover part of the domestic deficits.[23] This tolerance accentuated the corruption of the administration. In 1880, China imported more than 6500 tons of opium, the major part of which was produced in India, but as of this date, domestic farming was increasingly substituted for imports, by diffusing the opium addiction amongst small farmers and peasants, who were able to grow the product and consume up to a quarter of their own production.[24] The principal areas of production were in the southwest, in the very humid basin of Sichuan where the opium was primarily used as a remedy against malaria, dysentery and chills. In 1883, the Consul, Bodard, estimated the raw opium production of the province to be around 11 400 tons, or twice the amount of Chinese drug imports. A resident of Chongqing, Bodard observed in 1908 that 60 per cent of the fields were seeded with poppy, that a third of the city residents and a quarter of the peasants had become drug addicts. Hosie, the English Consul, himself settled in Chengdu in 1903, estimated that half of the adult male population consumed opium in the 500 opium dens in the city, but that this habit was seen in only 15 per cent of the peasants. According to Hosie, opium den clients mainly met in well-appointed merchant surroundings: 90 per cent of the civil servants and 80 per cent of the merchants of Chengdu were taking opium. At Chongqing, Bodard observed, however, that the smokers also included those of the lower classes: for the coolies, the palanquin drivers, the boatmen of the Yangtze, opium provided a stimulant for physical effort, even though they were consuming a drug that had been greatly adulterated, in rustic opium dens and not in luxurious establishments.[25] In the South of Sichuan, the high plateau of Yunnan-Guizhou, with its mountain-top tropical climate, also favoured poppy farming, and quickly came to occupy more than a third of the arable fields in Yunnan in 1875 and one half by 1900, according to the French Consul at Kunming, Auguste François.[26] Sichuan, Yunnan and Guizhou released the drug through the great artery of the Yangtze river. As of 1880, the English Consul at Yichang, the transit harbour part way along the long river, estimated the annual production of these three provinces to be around 14 900 tons of raw opium.[27]

The poppy harvest, which was between two and four times more profitable than wheat, was quickly expanded to other regions where it constituted an important base for local budgets: Shanxi, Henan, Shaanxi, Zhili around Peking, Eastern Mongolia and the Liaodong Peninsula in Manchuria. The price of domestic opium, inferior to a third of Indian opium, stimulated the demand and supply of drugs on the national market. At the beginning of the twentieth century, the opium harvest surpassed 22 000 tons, four times the illicit world production in 1895. China had at least 15 million smokers, who absorbed 95 per cent of world consumption, and the value of the interregional opium commerce surpassed that of rice and salt.[28]

Up until 1949, the poppy culture occupied approximately 10 million farmers and the traffic of drugs about 500 000 people.[29] The use of drugs had a great effect despite the reinforcement of prohibition, which was tightened by increasingly complex and severe legislation, in 1839, 1850 and 1870. However, this legal arsenal was used only sporadically to punish those involved, in a general context of opium importation legalization and of acceleration of domestic production.[30]

The Chinese experience of progressive population intoxication illustrates the limitation, of prohibition policies in a situation of increasing drug supply, stimulated by the freedom of trade, which facilitated the relationship between legal and illegal commerce. The conflicts between producer and consumer countries, whether they were manipulated by the colonial power or surmounted in the framework of national production in 1880, did not reduce the consumption of drugs, without doubt emphasized in the Chinese case by the corruption of values and regulation which reigned over the traditional society. The only difference lies in the monopolization of the added value from production and trafficking, which allowed for the quick accumulation of capital, without guaranteeing the efficiency of its allocation. Since the profits came from both national opium production and from trafficking, the prohibition policy may have succumbed to tolerance and to the status quo.

The decisive historical turning point came when there was an explosion of supply and a liberalization of trade, two parallel phenomena facing the prohibition policy which are mirrored in the international drug situation in the 1990s.

But in the nineteenth century, far from being the arm of the poor, opium was a strong driving force for colonial accumulation. The instructions of the British plenipotentiary government in charge of negotiating the Treaty of Nanking in 1841–42 are quite clear on this point. Sir H. Pottinger was responsible, after having settled the Treaty, for obtaining the legalization of the opium commerce by developing the following argument:

'Experience shows that it is entirely beyond the power of the Chinese government to prevent the introduction of opium in China ... While the opium commerce is prohibited by law, it is inevitably replaced by fraud and violence ... Her Majesty's government does not make any request with regards to this matter since it does not have the right to. The Chinese government is entirely free to prohibit the importation, if it chooses to, and the British subjects engaged in the smuggling commerce should be subject to the consequences of their act. But it is preferable that we take advantage of each favourable occasion to convince with energy the Chinese plenipotentiaries, in China's interest, to modify the Chinese legislation on this matter and to legally regulate a commerce which no prohibition may prevent.'[31]

In a 'private conversation' with the Chinese plenipotentiary Qiying, Sir H. Pottinger raised this question: the smoking habit had become a deep rooted vice for the population and no prohibition would have been able to hinder it. Was it not preferable to legalize importation and to stop smuggling? With the whole of the opium production from India being imported to China, was it not natural for China to try to discourage domestic farming? The use of tobacco, legalized in England, produced a revenue for the Crown.[32] These arguments were developed in a memorandum addressed to the Chinese plenipotentiary, which explained the advantages of a control system, of tolerance and of opium taxation similar to the commercial law on alcohol in western countries.

The installation of state monopolies of opium in the group of southeast Asian colonies, except for the Philippines, was therefore inspired by these principles. A series of recent works have shown the decisive contribution of opium revenues to colonial accumulations. In Singapore, the lease-farming of opium to Chinese merchants represented more than 40 per cent of the domestic budgetary resources during the greater part of the nineteenth century. The population included many drug addicts, to the extent that the expenses in opium for the leaf planters corresponded, even into the 1920s, to 60 per cent of their daily income.[33] In Java, the Dutch Company of the West Indies introduced an average of 56 tons of raw opium per year, between 1619 and 1799, and the colonial order in the nineteenth century came to be based more, at the outset, on opium revenue than on Dutch administrators' plans.[34] The case of the *Régie Française de l'opium*, created in Indochina by the governor Paul Doumer, remains as the most well-known. The opium monopoly amounted to 20 per cent of the general budget income of the colony during the entire period of 1899–1916, and 30–40 per cent when the war of 1914–18 reduced the contribution of the metropolis.

At the colonial Congress of 1908, the possibility of suppressing opium was judged by A. de Pouvourville not only as 'a ruin' for the public finances of Indochina, but also 'useless and even dangerous, since the addiction to opium will not be immediately eliminated, this abolition will only stimulate drug smuggling'. The state-owned control of opium, whose receipts surpassed those of alcohol and salt, thus greatly financed Vietnam's infrastructure.[35] The railway link from Yunnan to Tonkin was conceived as a result of the drug and tin needs, which constituted the principal purchases of French Indochina in China. According to Paul Butel 'the acknowledged objective' of the French in the construction of this railway, 'was to be able to capture a more considerable portion of the drug export on the one hand, to satisfy the needs of the French authority for control of opium in Indochina, and on the other, to participate in the drug commerce in China'. The French Consul at Kunming, Auguste François, in charge of establishing the route of this railway, proved to be very sceptical about the financial basis of this enterprise.[36] By the turn of the century, the importance of opium to the Far East colonial enterprises tended to generalize drug use among the military and overseas administrators themselves. For example, a police report of 1905 puts at more than 40 per cent the number of opium smokers among the officers of the French marine corps.[37]

This experience of effective colonial management in the production, trade and consumption of narcotics to the benefit of colonial governments contradicted the increasingly critical voice of the international community with regard to the drug. China had operated a painful revision policy following its defeat by Japan in 1895 and since the new western intervention of 1900, provoked by the upheaval of the Boxers. In the reform policy adopted in 1901, the Manchu dynasty launched an efficient short-term campaign against the use of opium and the farming of poppies, by mobilizing the local administration as well as the public. The Middle Empire obtained the support of the British House of Commons which unanimously condemned the traffic of opium as morally indefensible. In 1908, the British government committed itself to reducing exports of Indian opium. In the space of five years, Chinese opium production decreased by one half according to official statistics. Many opium dens were closed down, their clients registered with the police and the pipes confiscated and destroyed. Faced with an increasing scarcity of the drug, certain consumers turned to substitute products, often more dangerous ones, such as 'Jesus' opium – morphine-based pills freely imported and often commercialized by Chinese Christians.[38]

At the initiative of the United States, the Shanghai Conference, held in 1909, gathered all the great powers together to contemplate means of prohibiting opium and its derivatives in the countries and possessions of the Far East. The conference condemned the production and the traffic of drugs and invited governments to criminalize them, but the conference's resolutions were simple declarations of principle and had no value in international law. Negotiations continued within the framework of three conferences at The Hague (1911–1914), then, after the war of 1914–18, at two conferences in Geneva in 1924. It would be useful here to consider the debates at these conferences as they illustrate the increasing gap between the desire for a prohibition policy and the detrimental consequences for economic interests.[39]

With the first conference at The Hague in December 1911, English representatives were instructed to express reservations on all of the decisions concerning the commerce or the use of opium in the Indies and in all other British property. The English and French representatives did not agree with the American position, which tended to consider opium to be used for smoking outside of the production country, as contraband. The resolutions of the conference on the opium trade were always limited by the final Convention text: it only considered 'packages superior to five kilograms', and it had no obligatory character nor was it consistent about any delaying of its applications.

The authorities who had their possessions in the Far West hence refused to adopt any effective and immediate prohibition measures. The two conferences at The Hague in December 1912 and in June 1914 reinforced this position. Whereas a certain number of States refused to sign the Convention, others such as Great Britain, France, Persia and Siam formulated reservations related to its implications for their drug production and trade.

The negotiations restarted the day after the end of the First World War. The pact of nations, incorporated in the Treaty of Versailles, made the League of Nations responsible for controlling the application of measures outlined in the Convention of The Hague. The Opium Consultative Commission was created to that effect. According to its constitution, this body was grounded in reality 'by considering the huge interests and often divergent ones, that are engaged in the trafficking of opium', and by estimating that a prohibition of its abusive use was impossible. The only feasible policy towards the illegal entry of products such as morphine or cocaine consisted of 'controlling the consumption and limiting the abuses as much as possible, at least as long as the poppy was still cultivated in considerable proportions and that we could procure opium'. The president of the medical Commission of India declared that in his country:

> 'We consume opium as we do tea or tobacco. Opium consists of a drug for the worker compelled to hard work, for soldiers who must face long marches, and even for animals. Its use may have unfortunate consequences during youth, but not after forty years old, when the energy tends to decrease. It does not have an effect on crime such as cocaine.'[40]

In these conditions, it is not surprising that the American proposal to reserve the legitimate use of opium for medical and scientific use was contested by the Indian, French and English delegates. The production and the use of opium were 'temporarily maintained in a certain number of Far Eastern countries'.

In 1924, the two conferences in Geneva were unable to achieve the adoption of common measures aiming to limit the use of drugs in these same countries. The break-up of China after the revolution, aborted in 1911, favoured the continuance of poppy farming and the consumption of opium, which largely financed the armies of the war lords and provided one half of the revenues of certain provinces. One of the chiefs of the Guangxi group, Huang Shaohong, thus estimated in his memoirs that 'in all of the conflicts between war lords, which wounded all of the provinces in China during many decades, we may confirm that all had a relation with opium'.[41] The English delegate in Geneva quoted a report of the International Association against opium, based in Peking, which estimated the Chinese production at about 15 000 tons per year, in other words 90 per cent of the world's production at the time.[42] The American delegate outlined the terms of the responsibility of the colonial powers, who refrained, in the Chinese situation, from putting into place the measures outlined in the Convention of The Hague: 'There should not be one morality for the West and another for the East. All that is forbidden and severely punished in Western countries should not be legitimate, nor defended and developed in the East.'[43]

Since China was not able to observe its international commitment with regard to prohibition, England, France and the Netherlands abstained from all efforts in this matter. Even the harbours and territories leased from China became centres for the continuing drugs industry. The most spectacular case was that of the French concession of Shanghai, where the great godfathers of the secret societies lived. Huang Jingrong, Zhang Xiaoling and Du Yuesheng were respected members of the community and, at the same time, gang leaders of the drugs, gambling and prostitution trades, businesses which prospered thanks to the passive corruption of the French services. Joseph Shieh, a former official responsible for the political police service in the French concession of Shanghai, described the godfathers of that time in the following terms:

'Zhang Xiaoling, the most educated of the three, who was on very good terms with the governor of Zhejiang, Lu Yongxiang, served as an intermediary between the war lords and the two other godfathers, Du Yuesheng and Huang Jingrong (he himself an inspector-detective of the French police) to facilitate the transport of opium, by land or by sea. In 1924, he even founded an Insurance company, called the Sanxing (the company with the three-fold development), with the agreement of the general Consul of France of the time, Mr. Koeklin, and of Captain Fiori, and with his two accomplices, in order to guarantee the drug against the risks of robbery or accident. The traffickers in Canton greatly adhered to this which was, for the gang leaders, the true kick-start of their fortunes. They constructed two great buildings for their offices, at 216 Wagner Street, and shared their responsibilities. Zhang was in charge of public relations with the war lords, Huang covered the smuggling activities inside the French police, and Du took care of

16

public relations with the French authorities; Du held the best relations with Mr. Verdier, director of the French municipality, as well as with Captain Fiori.'[44]

If the reluctance of the Asian colonial powers with regard to the prohibition was essentially a consequence of the fiscal loss that such a policy would bring about, the arguments of the colonial administrators were manifested differently. The Chinese represented about 90 per cent of opium smokers in the Far Eastern territories and possessions.[45] The Opium Investigations Commission, sent in 1929 by the League of Nations, noted the major role played by these immigrants in the economic development of certain territories. Very strict control on the use of opium, or its total suppression, may have stopped the flow of workers necessary for domestic economies, or even provoked an immediate exodus with disastrous effects. This argument was borrowed by the British North Borneo Co. and by the Netherlands government which declared that: 'if the use of opium came to be entirely restricted, it would become if not impossible, at least very difficult to have our work force. The general prosperity would then become affected by this measure.'[46] The administrators of British Malaysia, including the Straits Settlements, underlined the 'disastrous repercussions that all obstacles to the free flow of Chinese workers would have on the domestic economic situation'. Of the 2 million Chinese people living in Malaysia, in other words one-fifth of the total population, there were at least 400 000 opium smokers, 70 per cent of whom had developed this habit locally.[47] The argument is particularly cynical when we know that, at the same time, the opium monopoly assured one-third of the revenues of the British Straits Settlements of Singapore.[48]

Thus, the resolutions of the Hague Convention essentially concerned the metropolitan territories, as the colonial governments were careful to conserve the revenues they gained from opium. The governmental monopolies did not allow for a decrease either in smuggling activity or, in the majority of cases, in opium consumption, as was hoped for during the first conference of Geneva.[49] This very lucrative policy of tolerance caused great indignation: 'If opium is so productive and so inoffensive', as one reads in the *Bulletin of Missions*, 'why not organize in European metropolises the sale and the State monopoly of a product we offer to colonies? ... It is criminal to offer others the diffusion of a vice that we repudiate at home.'[50] But these protests did not alter the situation in the least, despite international efforts towards regulation and prohibitions. The considerable economic interests, related to colonial or predatory states – such as China had become during the Guomindang regime – stimulated the licit or illicit production and distribution of drugs.[51]

The mirror of history thus reflects the six levers of international drug trafficking and consumption that are still relevant in the 1990s: (i) the expansion and diversification of drug supply; (ii) crises and shocks caused by socio-economic change threatening the structure of society; (iii) commercial globalization; (iv) economic interests related to the rapid accumulation of capital and the modification of terms of trade; (v) the direct or indirect influence of financial matters on state power; and (vi) the multiplication of low-intensity conflicts. These six elements are self-perpetuating: the rise in the number of conflicts and the existence of state debt generate exceptional financial requirements that may combine to favour an increase in drug production and trafficking.

Notes

1 Report of the GAFI (Financial Action Group): *The Fight Against Capital Laundering*, Paris, La Documentation Française, 1990.
2 Cf. *Le Monde*, 16 June 1995. The turnover of the arms trade represented more than 21.7 billion dollars in 1994.
3 Michel Schiray, 'Drug procedures: three levels, five logics', *Futuribles*, March 1994, p. 28. In the case of Pakistani heroin, 90 per cent of the turnover takes place in Europe and in the United States, cf. *World Drug Report*, United Nations Drug Control Programme, Oxford University Press, 1997, p. 131.

4 *Futuribles,* Review, Geopolitics of drugs, special issue, March 1994, pp. 89–90.

5 David Owen, *British Opium Policy in India and China,* Yale University Press, 1934.

6 Jonathan Spence, 'Opium smoking in Qing China', *Chinese Roundabout, Essays in History and Culture,* New York, WW Norton and Co., 1992.

7 Jonathan Spence, *The Search for Modern China,* New York, WW Norton and Co., 1990, pp. 129–31; Spencer. 'Opium smoking'.

8 Cf. Chantal Descours-Gatin, *Quand l'opium finançait la colonisation,* Paris, Ed. L'Harmattan, 1992, p. 10.

9 Spence, 'Opium smoking'.

10 Spence, *The Search,* p. 129.

11 Wang Adine, *La Chine et le problème de l'opium,* Paris, A. Pedone, 1933.

12 Léonard P. Adams, 'la Chine, berceau du fléau de l'opium', in Alfred MacCoy, *La politique de l'héroine en Asie du sud-est,* Paris, Flammarion, 1980.

13 Cf. Paul Butel, *L'opium: Histoire d'une fascination,* Paris, Ed. Plon, 1995, p. 70.

14 Cf. Louis Dermigny, *La Chine et l'Occident: le commerce à Canton au 18 ème siècle, 1719–1833,* Paris, Imprimerie Nationale, 1964, 3 volumes, p. 1301. This thesis consists of the most researched analysis with regard to the role of the drug in the Chinese foreign trade from the eighteenth century until the beginning of the nineteenth century.

15 Spence, *The Search,* p. 129.

16 Spence, 'Opium smoking', p. 234.

17 MacCoy, *La politique de l'héroine,* p. 589.

18 Owen, *British Opium Policy,* p. 80.

19 Spence, *The Search,* p. 149.

20 Wang Adine, *La Chine,* pp. 32–3.

21 Butel, *L'opium,* pp. 114–15 and 153.

22 Spence, 'Opium smoking', p. 251.

23 Ibid., p. 252.

24 Ibid., p. 237.

25 Paul Butel, *L'opium,* pp. 202–3.

26 Dominique Liabeuf and Jorge Svartzman, *L'oeil du consul, Auguste François en Chine,* Paris, Ed du Chêne, 1989, p. 21.

27 David Owen, quoted in Paul Butel, *L'opium,* p. 90.

28 MacCoy, *La politique de l'héroine,* pp. 472–4.

29 Yu Xiaodong and Li Yundong, *Da jin du* [The drug prohibition], Beijing, Yuanjie chubanshe, 1993, p. 234.

30 Spence, 'Opium smoking', p. 243.
31 Wang Adine, *La Chine*, pp. 52–3.
32 Ibid., p. 61.
33 Carl A. Trocki, *Opium and Empire: Chinese Society in Colonial Singapore, 1800–1910*, New York, Cornell University Press, 1991; James Francis Warren, *Rickshaw Coolie: A People's History of Singapore, 1880–1940*, Singapore, Oxford University Press, 1986, p. 246.
34 James R. Rush, *Opium to Java: Revenue Farming and Chinese Enterprise in Colonial Indonesia, 1860–1910*, New York, Cornell University Press, 1990, p. 27.
35 Chantal Descours-Gatin, *Quand l'opium finançait*, pp. 223–4 and 245.
36 Butel, *L'opium*, p. 205; Dominique Liabeuf and Jorge Svartzman, *L'oeil du consul*.
37 Butel, *L'opium*. p. 352; Chantal Descours-Gatin, *Quand l'opium finançait*.
38 Spence, 'Opium smoking', p. 250.
39 On his conferences, see Wang Adine, *La Chine*.
40 On all of the negotiations and interventions of the delegates, see Wang Adine, *La Chine*.
41 Dong Yimin, 'Le problème de l'opium dans la région du sud-ouest de la Chine pendant les années 1920 et 1930', Doctorate thesis under the direction of Lucien Bianco, EHESS, Paris, 1997.
42 Wang Adine, *La Chine*, p. 113.
43 Ibid., p. 135.
44 Joseph Shieh and Marie Holzman, *Dans le jardin des aventuriers*, Paris, Seuil/Mémoire, 1995, p. 71. The best study on the relation of drug trafficking and organized crime in Shanghai is that of Brian Martin: *The Shanghai Green Gang, Politics and Organized Crime, 1917–1937*, Berkeley, University of California Press, 1996.
45 Wang Adine, *La Chine* p. 108.
46 Ibid., p. 212.
47 Ibid., p. 215.
48 Ibid., p. 218.
49 Ibid., pp. 225–6.
50 Ibid., pp. 214–15.
51 See the communication of Lucien Bianco and Alan Baumler at the conference 'Opium in East Asian History, 1830–1945', University of Toronto, York University, May 1997 in: Timothy Brook and Bob Tadashi Wakebashi (editors), *Opium Regimes: China Britain and Japan 1839–1952*, Berkeley, University of California Press, 2000. See also the thesis of Dong Yiming, 'Etude sur le problème de l'opium dans la région du sud-ouest chinois dans les années 1920–1930', under the direction of Lucien Bianco, EHESS, Paris, 1997.

2

Drugs and Post-Communism:
The Chinese Case

The capitalist unification of the planet which has been at work since the collapse of the Eastern bloc, the end of the Soviet Union and the adoption of the market economy in China, allowed for the reopening of the former silk roads, which were also those used for drugs.[1] According to the United Nations Drug Control Program (UNDCP), world opium production has increased two-fold since the break-up of the USSR.[2] Eurasia is no longer split by an iron curtain or by Sino–Soviet border tension, while the former Soviet Union is weakly recomposed as a Russian state – the Confederation of Independent States (CIS) – and in an Islamic Fundamentalism reinforcement context. The multiplication of conflicts among Sunni, Shiite and Orthodox populations, from the Balkans to Central Asia, has reinforced the tendency towards militarization. The disintegration or the collapse of communist parties, which were based on an accumulation and management of political capital, has given birth to a new logic of power, founded on the nationalist re-conversion of the bureaucratic elite and on their accelerated re-appropriation of public capital. This dynamic simultaneously favours military influence, which appears as the shield or the spearhead for fragile authorities, and local or sectorial bureaucracies. The latter reinforce tendencies toward economic feudalism. In their new managerial roles, local authorities or central authorities, owners of a monopoly, aim to maximize enterprise or activity incomes that are under their control by minimizing the risks of external competition. Far from breaking monopolies, the institutional structures of decentralization have multiplied them. The institutional structures favour the creation of a profit economy without competition which, allied to the coercive means of the army, constitutes an ideal environment for the development of a Mafia, in the actual context of the globalization of trade.

This situation, which prevails in southeast Europe,[3] is particularly visible in the case of the former USSR, where the annual turnover of drug trafficking is estimated at US$6 billion and where drug dealings increased by 40 per cent in 1994.[4] Since the laundering of drug money is not illegal, more than half of the top twenty-five Russian banks maintain a relation with organized crime, according to one CIA report.[5] With the shadow economy employing 6 million people – about 9 per cent of the active population – the criminal networks controlled 46 per cent of the distribution of goods imported illegally,[6] and the Russian Mafia had 53 billion dollars in their Swiss accounts.[7] Moscow estimates a capital flow to Switzerland, along with Austria, Cyprus and North America, that reached about 25 billion dollars at the beginning of 1994.[8] But one year later, the *Izvestiya* quoted a high official according to whom the amount would apparently reach about 100 billion dollars.[9] Most of the funds came from petroleum sales or public goods commissions. According to the Russian Home Office, criminal groups controlled 35 per cent of the trade volume and racketeered between 10 and 20 per cent of the imports–exports.[10] In Moscow, it represented more than half of the real estate market.[11] The constitution of these criminal monopolies rests upon the extensive exercise of violence, which targeted 40 000 victims in 1994 in Russia alone.[12] The judicial legislature estimates that a large part of the initial capital of legitimate small retail outlets, boutiques, restaurants or fruit and vegetable markets, is suspected to have come from drug trafficking.[13] In October 1994, the murder of the journalist Dimitri Kholodov, who investigated a network of gun and drug smugglers organized by the army and the Russian secret services between Tadjikistan and the troops stationed in Berlin, triggered off a wave of protests in Moscow against the Defence Minister Pavel Gratchev, locally known as 'Pacha-Mercedes'. The Vice-Minister of Defence, Matveï Bourlakov, was finally forced to resign.[14]

All of the elements were therefore reassembled to transform the CIS into a new drugs power. Increasingly used as a transit zone for opium and heroin in the Golden Crescent, and established as the first world producer of opium products in 1994, the CIS is also potentially the first world producer of hashish; 3 million hectares of marijuana grow on its territories in a wild state.[15] The poppy culture has developed in the Central Asia States, in Uzbekistan where the yield from one acre of cultivated poppy is about twenty times higher than a cotton hectare,[16] and in Tadjikistan, which was ripped apart like its neighbour Afghanistan by civil war. In the Central Asia States, industrial production has fallen by half since the end of the Soviet era and unemployment of the active population has reached almost 35 per cent, according to the estimate of the World Bank. It is not surprising if 'the drug is what works in the country's market', according to an anti-narcotics division responsible to the Kirghiz Ministry of Interior: 'it solves all of the problems. People consume more and more, grow them, import and export them. If you have the means, you may even pay the Russian guards of the border to deliver your opium by helicopter.'[17] The considerable stocks of guns and arms which were accumulated up to the end of the USSR may be used to trade in exchange for drugs, and this may feed local conflicts. The army, and more generally the military-industrial infrastructure, severely hit by the great recession of the 1990s, have used their new political prerogatives to ensure the continuation of smuggling.[18]

These developments have direct repercussions for the European Union: the reunified Germany where, for example, more than 12 000 enterprises have been privatized in three years, has become a privileged field for eastern Mafia investments. The German information service estimates that US$30 billion have been laundered in their country, by bringing US$3 billion into the banks.[19] According to other sources, Mafia groups had recycled DM72 billions in the ex-German Democratic Republic by the end of 1994, which represents one-third of foreign investments carried out after the fall of the Berlin wall.[20] The scale of these transfers, which are by nature very difficult to evaluate, reflects the considerable development of the shadow economy, but also shows the necessity of these profits being deposited in the great industrialized countries which also constitute the principal drug markets.

The rapid accumulation of capital passes from the production country and through the transit country, and essentially comes back to the wealthy countries, which are the winners in economic terms. The tide of narco-dollars is thus replicating the tide of petro-dollars, without fundamentally modifying the terms of trade. In each case, the production zones are forced to buy arms from industrialized countries, for use in debilitating local conflicts.

The rise of drug trafficking and consumption in China

If the case of the former USSR shows to what extent post-communism presents a favourable field for the expansion of drug trafficking, the case of China, less known today, is just as significant. Despite the fact that an official communist party remains in power, China's transition towards a market economy, much more advanced than that of Russia, has favoured a new balance which in fact is quite similar to that of its great former Soviet brother. The communist party converted itself into patriotism, the bureaucracy into business, and the army – which has become a shareholder in the reforms – appears to be the last shield of a weakened authority. The economic feudalism of regional leaders, the tendency to maximize the entrepreneurial profits under their territorial control by minimizing competition, are fed by the under-development of the transport infrastructure and the resurgence of local mentalities and networks as a refuge against a discredited central power.

Finally China adjoins two principal zones of opium by-product production. The Golden Crescent, where Afghanistan produced 3200 to 3300 tons of opium in 1994 and Pakistan 30–40 tons of heroin, is adjacent to the great province of Xinjiang and borders Tadjikistan, Kirghiztan and Kazakhstan, which are the principal neighbours of China in Central Asia. Beside the Golden Triangle, the province of Yunnan shares a border of 4060 km with three states: Burma, producer of 2500 tons of opium and 230 tons of heroin in 1995; Laos, where the yearly production is estimated at 200 tons of raw opium; and Vietnam, an important transit zone.[21]

Drug trafficking and consumption rose considerably in China after 1989. If 70–80 per cent of European heroin consumption came from the Golden Crescent via Turkey and the Balkan routes, about 60 per cent of the heroin consumed in the United States came from the Golden Triangle, according to data from the American services. These drugs transit through China, and have a massive impact by feeding an explosion of local consumption which is today spread throughout the country. The Public Security Office of Yunnan, the principal centre of drug trafficking, estimated in 1994 that about 60 per cent of Burmese heroin came from China. The new networks of the *Chinese white* took over an increasing part of the American market by offering a purer and less expensive heroin than that of competitors.[22]

The very strict prohibition policy, which had resulted in an almost total eradication of the opium by-product consumption in China in the 1950s, 1960s and 1970s, was not able to halt its resumption. In fact, rather than prohibition, it would be more correct to speak of an extraordinary permissiveness on the part of the authorities in the 1980s, while poppy farming, production, trafficking and consumption of heroin developed, starting in the neighbouring countries of the Golden Triangle. According to the regulations of 1986, the consumption of opium by-products was liable to a 200 yuan fine (US$25) and a 15 day detention. Poppy cultivation or the production of narcotics was subject to the same penalty, with a fine this time of approximately 3000 yuan (US$360). The return of the prohibition occurred with the law of December 1990, which punishes, with a 15 year prison sentence, life imprisonment or, in the worst cases, the death penalty, for smuggling, trafficking or manufacturing more than one kilo of opium, more than 50 grams of heroin or a specific quantity of other drugs.[23]

This late legislation was not able to stop the increase in the number of drug addicts, although definite figures remain difficult to verify. According to the first official statements, there were 250 000 'registered' heroin addicts, 40 000 of whom came from Yunnan and 40 000 from Guangxi.[24] Guangxi has 1600 km of coast and shares a border with Vietnam: 82 per cent of the heroin data and 70 per cent of those for opium were gathered in these two provinces, through which a great part of the drug consumed in China is chanelled, or exported, mainly via Hong Kong networks.[25] Then the Public Security Minister, Tao Siju, announced in 1995 that the number of people registered as drug addicts had increased to a level of 380 000,[26] 100 000 of whom were from the province of Sichuan, which itself has a population of 110 million.[27] The following year, the same sources produced a figure of 520 000 registered drug addicts, 80 per cent of whom were adolescents.[28] But the experts estimate that the number of drug addicts is at least four times higher than the number who are registered. In Peking, for example, 4545 drug addicts are declared, whereas our estimated number of consumers was 22 000.[29] One study has shown that the number of drug addicts could be ten times higher than the registered figure, which may be true, taking local figures into account.[30] Only the province of Guangxi, which borders that of Yunnan, today admits that there are 300 000 drug addicts registered for a population of 46 million.[31]

At the regional level, the examples of Yunnan and of Guangdong are quite eloquent. As of 1989, the authorities of Yunnan estimate that the 'fans of the n°4' (*si hao ge*) or those that are 'hooked' (*yin junzi*) on heroin represent 108 000 in a population of 36.5 million. This evaluation is judged to be 'quite modest' according to the local service experts.[32] Trafficking and consumption developed in some commercial cities on the Sino–Burmese border, where heroin was freely sold at the beginning of the 1980s in the 'drug streets' (*duping jie*) or 'the n°4 streets' (*si hao jie*).[33] Drug addiction quickly reached a significant level in those regions populated with non-Chinese-influenced people that are found on both sides of the border. We may give as an example a village with 33 families and 112 residents in which 22 young men out of 28 take heroin.[34] In the Dehong prefecture, which faces the Burmese Kokang, in the North of the Golden Triangle, the number of heroin addicts went from 18 in 1982 to 15 000 at the beginning of the 1990s. The border city of Ruili, along the famous Burma road, could count at the same time about 3000 heroin addicts according to the health services.[35] Yunnan seems to have realigned itself with its 1949 past, when it counted 2 million opium addicts in a population of 16 million (12.5 per cent). In the capital of the province, Kunming, at that time we would estimate 50 000 opium addicts in a population of 300 000 (one out of six people), 1670 opium dens and 6968 traffickers.[36]

The case of Guangdong, at the other extreme, illustrates the ties that link traffic and consumption. At the beginning of the 1980s, the province of Guangdong, the spearhead of the political opening towards Hong Kong and the international market, was used as a place for heroin transits from the Golden Triangle. The first trafficking business was discovered at Shantou, the capital for the Chaozhou Chinese, in a Thai plane. From 1983 to 1984, there were a few dozen cases, and by 1992 more than 200.[37] During the same year, a publication from Hong Kong, quoting the Public Security officials of Guangdong, estimated between 500 000 and 600 000 drug addicts in that province where the population was 65 million people.[38] If this is the case, the hard drug users of Guangdong by far surpassed those of Italy (260 000 for a population of 57 million), the European country most affected by heroin.[39]

According to the authorities, the drug addicts are actually spread across 700 districts and 17 provinces,[40] but internal documents from 1992 reveal that the worst offences linked to drugs affected as many as 27–31 Chinese provinces and municipalities.[41] By dividing up these local data, the official data and internal documents, Dali L. Yang, whose study was the first one devoted to the renewal of drug addiction in China, estimated the number of addicts as being 'at least a million and certainly more'.[42] According to his evaluation, Yunnan had more than 100 000 drug addicts by 1987: in a study done at the time on 65 000 Yunnanese, 3.5 per cent of the people interrogated were identified as drug addicts, the majority of them addicted to heroin. The rate of opium by-product dependence is much higher in the region of Ruili, on the Sino–Burmese border: it involved between 6 and 12 per cent of the villages' population at the beginning of the 1990s.[43] If one considers the example of Guangdong, where the number of addicts doubled in 1990 and redoubled during the first half of 1991,[44] it is true that Yunnan, Guangxi and the other Chinese provinces have followed the same trend. The Chinese civil service estimates, which privately counted 2.5 million drug addicts, therefore seem modest.[45] These numbers remain quite low relative to the mass population, but it places China as the first among world consumer countries and Third World countries, placing it before Pakistan (where 1.5 million are drug addicts in a population of 120 million), which yearly absorbs about 70–80 tons of heroin.[46] According to 'the most conservative' official estimate, heroin consumption amounts to an order of 40 tons yearly in China.[47] Drug trafficking, including all products, generates a yearly turnover of about 30 billion yuan (US$3.6 billion).[48]

Developments in the 1990s show that countries involved in the transit of drugs have a tendency to become massive consumers, as is confirmed by the example of Thailand,[49] which has at least 500 000 heroin addicts, and of Vietnam, where there are estimated to be about 200 000. Even though the majority of the heroin turnover is in the European and American markets – especially in the United States with about 600 000 heroin addicts – Asian opium by-products are principally consumed in Asia,[50] which helps to explain the gap between the production and consumption estimates given by the Arche Summit Report.[51]

Chinese opium addiction is mainly seen among rural people – in Guizhou, in Sichuan, and in Mongolia – but the huge majority of drug addicts are young men between the ages of 15 and 30,[52] hooked on heroin n°4 from Burma, which they prefer to smoke mixed with tobacco instead of absorbing it through intravenous injections. This practice, however, has increased during the 1990s, evidenced by the 150 000 to 200 000 estimated HIV positive people in China at the end of 1996, more than 76 per cent of whom contracted the disease by injecting heroin into themselves. Most of the registered cases are originally from the province of Yunnan, along the Golden Triangle. Hard drug consumption has thus become the principal cause of the spread of AIDS, which may strike 10 million Chinese in the first decade of the twenty-first century, in the absence of counter-measures.[53] The use of syringes has also spread the Hepatitis C virus, as in Guangxi.[54] The impact of drug addiction on public health is therefore very serious.

Heroin consumption first became a fashion phenomenon in the rich districts of the cities: sons of executives, artists and young businessmen represented about one-third of drug addicts.[55] It quickly reached the young unemployed and young labourers, then spread to the rural areas, from the neighbouring zones of the Golden Triangle to the trafficking regions: in the South the provinces of Yunnan, Guangxi, Guizhou and Guangdong, and towards the North the provinces of Sichuan, Gansu, Ningxia and Xinjiang, and then Shaanxi and Shanxi at the very side of the ancient Silk Road. The data on opium by-products document this progression, despite the fact that the Chinese director of Interpol, Zhu Entao, contributed to its decrease, in 1994, through the reinforcement of anti-drug measures along the southeast border.[56] (Table 2.1). Trafficking has a tendency to develop today in the northwest, and especially in Xinjiang, the neighbouring countries of Afghanistan, Pakistan, Kazakhstan and Tadjikistan,[57] with a diversification in favour of *ice*

Table 2.1 The stuggle against drug trafficking in China 1981–1996

Year	Confiscation of opium (kg)	Confiscation of heroin (kg)	Number of traffickers arrested (Chinese and foreign)
1981–82	no data	no data	no data
1983	5.25	0.05	10
1984	30	no data	4
1985	50	6.7	15
1986	112.7	24.1	32
1987	137.5	38.7	74
1988	239.1	166.2	188
1989	269.4	488.3	749
1990	782	1632	5612
1991	1980	1959	18479
1992	2660	4489	28000
1993	3354	4459	40834
1994	1700	3881	38033
1995	1110	2736	73730
1996	1700	4000	87000

Sources: from 1981 to 1992, Dali L.Yang, *The Journal of Contemporary China*, Fall 1993. For the confiscation of heroin in 1991, *People's Daily*, 23 March 1992 in SWB BBC Asia-Pacific, 4 April 1992. For 1993 and 1994, *Beijing Information*, 2 January 1995 and 11 December 1995; *China Daily*, 28 March 1995 and 23 June 1995; Zhongguo xinwen she, 4 July 1996 in SWB BBC Far East, 10 July 1996; Xinhua, 17 January 1997 in SWB BBC Asia Pacific, 21 January 1997.

(metamphetamine), produced from ephedrine, of which the main world producers are the Chinese. From 1991 to 1996, 4.7 tons of *ice* were produced, essentially in the provinces of Guangdong and Fujian.[58] Trafficking also has a tendency to become globalized, towards Russia which shares 4000 km of open borders with China, but also to Mexico, where some companies legally imported the Chinese forerunners of metamphetamines, so as to re-export them towards illegal *ice* laboratories in the United States.[59]

The new drugs war

Since 1994, there has been a noticeable emphasis on prohibition policy, launched in the aftermath of Tian'anmen. In November 1989, the State Affairs Council launched a national campaign with the objective of eradicating six social problems (liu haï): (i) prostitution; (ii) pornography; (ii) the kidnapping and trafficking of children and women; (iv) the production, consumption and trafficking of drugs; (v) gambling; and (vi) belief in superstitions. Consumption and trafficking continued to increase in 1989–90, especially in urban zones such as Guangdong, Zhejiang, Fujian or Peking. This revival of drug abuse can be attributed to the general disillusionment which followed the fall of the democratic movement and the policy of economic austerity.[60] In 1990, the State Council established a National Commission of Narcotics Control led by the Public Security Minister, Tao Siju. She is responsible for reinforcing legislative devices, formulating concrete proposals for policies and co-ordinating the activity of the sixteen administrations concerned. The drugs war, 'a question of life or death', was launched shortly afterwards, through the instigation of Jiang Zemin, the Secretary General of the party. Public trials and executions of traffickers are regularly organized on 26 June – the International Day against drugs – and 26 October in all of the provinces. This ritual takes on a particular dimension in Kunming, the capital of Yunnan, where thousands of people yearly attend the trial and mass execution of dozens of traffickers, generally very young people. The Yunnan tribunals condemned to death more than 240 people in 1990, 240 in 1991, 473 in 1993 and 466 in 1994.[61] At the national level, in 1993, 1410 death sentences or sentences to life imprisonment were pronounced for drug offences, according to the Narcotics Control Division,[62] representing an increase over the preceding year (1354).[63] The repression increased in 1994, with the execution of 1400 traffickers during the first three months of the year.[64] Most of the local data confirm that the drug war has continued ever since, and at the same level: on 26 June 1994, 46 drug traffickers were gunned down in Canton and 38 others in Sichuan.[65] During the second half of 1994, the services of Guangdong found 167 kg of heroin and 113 kg of opium and other drugs.[66] In April 1995, the governor, Zhu Shenlin, evoked the 'popular drug war', during a televised speech in the province of Guangdong, the transit region from the Golden Triangle for heroin destined for Hong Kong and the western markets. Zhu Shenlin denounced the extension of drug trafficking and consumption which struck in particular ten large cities, three of which are the special economic regions of Shenzhen, followed by Hong Kong, Zhuhai, Macao, and Shantou, the kingdom of the Chaozhou Chinese (Teochew). He emphasized the relationship between trafficking and prostitution, and the consequences of this situation for delinquency. Heroin addicts were invited to register so that they could be treated and traffickers were encouraged to hand themselves in to security organizations where they would be treated with mercy.[67] This campaign brought, within a few months, 19 000 drug addicts into rehabilitation centres, and captured 338 kg of heroin. The Canton policy dismantled an important network of drug traffickers, arresting 12 people and capturing 159.25 kg of heroin from the Golden Triangle destined for foreign countries.[68] On 16 May 1995, 51 traffickers were executed in the province of Guangdong,[69] but this did not reduce the trafficking, as was witnessed by the seizure of heroin in 1996 in the same province: 600 kg on 25 April at Shenzhen – the special economic zone on the border of Hong Kong, which has become a trafficking centre[70] – 137 kg a few days later, 42 kg on 8 May. On 31 May, the authorities once again discovered 312 kg of heroin escorted by two natives of Hong Kong in the Southwest of Yunnan[71], which provides evidence of the increasing size of the trafficking industry. On 26 June 1996, the international day for the fight against drugs was marked by public trials, mobilizing 1.75 million people, with the death sentence or life imprisonment being passed on 769 charged people and the executions of at least 260 traffickers, 59 of which were at Guangxi, 56 at Sichuan, 39 at Guangdong, 32 at Yunnan, 32 at Guizhou and 19 at Gansu.[72]

The size of this repression may be surprising at first sight, but it is nothing exceptional in China. Amnesty International records about 1500 officially announced death sentences annually in the districts known for drug offences, and estimates approximately 10 000 executions under common law.[73] In 1995, the Chinese government increased sentences, announcing 2500 executions.[74] In 1996, the authorities officially proceeded with 4367 executions, one-tenth of which (437) were drug traffickers.[75] If this proportion is representative, the drug abuse situation is increasingly coming closer to that which prevailed in 1949, when 18.6 per cent of the criminal cases in the country were related to drugs.[76] More than the actual number being executed, it is the proportion that is important here, and which is largely underestimated at the national level: the official *China Daily* announced, as we have seen, 466 executions of drug traffickers in 1994 solely for the province of Yunnan.[77]

Since 1994, new police army units have been allowed to infiltrate the large centres on the Sino–Burmese border. One notorious trafficker, Yang Maoxian, the brother of Yang Mao'an, who controlled the poppy and heroin production zone of Kokang, in the North of the Golden Triangle, was arrested on 8 May in the region of Wanding, on the border of the Burma road. Accused of having organized the trafficking of 270 kg of heroin in China since 1990, Yang Maoxian was sentenced to death and executed on 7 October 1994 with 16 accomplices, two of whom were local police officers and two who were provincial police officers from the coast of Fujian.[78] This would seem to have been the first case which concerned a drug godfather rather than just small traffickers: approximately 200 civil servants from the police, customs and security forces were detained during the arrest of Yang Maoxian. This fact underlines the extent of the official involvement in trafficking. The determination of the authorities would have resulted in a reduction in the heroin smuggling by half in the northern region of the Golden Triangle.[79]

This strict prohibition policy launched a national propaganda campaign on drug offences and the public destruction of drug stocks. In June 1992, the municipality of Kunming burnt a ton of heroin and four tons of opium; whereas the 150th anniversary of the Nankin Treaty was an opportunity for the authorities to celebrate once again 'the righteous fight against drugs' of commissioner Lin Zexu, long enshrined in the national communist pantheon. These 'burnings' took place periodically, sometimes in the exact place where Lin Zexu had burned the English opium stocks in 1839: in June 1997 in the little city of Humen, on the delta of the Pearls River, the Narcotics National Commission and the province of Guangdong organized as a highly publicized event the destruction of 300 kg of heroin and 100 kg of *ice*, in front of a monument in honour of prohibition, where two fists arise from the ground and break a gigantic opium pipe.[80] One week later, slightly less than a ton of heroin was burnt at Kunming, the capital of Yunnan.[81]

The police measures were followed by the establishment of 500 rehabilitation centres which treat 50 000 drug abusers, and 75 centres of 'work detoxification' which treat 30 000 people detained within the Chinese Gulag.[82] Will the war against drugs succeed in curbing the wave of heroin consumption developed by trafficking? Nothing is very certain. The President of the Popular Supreme Court, Ren Jianxin, insisted, in his 1996 report, on the rapid increase in the offences related to drugs, which represents an indubitable risk for the Chinese.[83] At the world conference in Naples on organized crime (November 1994), the Minister of Justice, Xiao Yang, pointed out the increasing influence of gangs and Mafia-type associations in China, which 'may infiltrate the actual economic sectors.'[84] These tendencies were confirmed by the national director of Interpol, Zhu Entao, and by the Public Security Minister, Tao Siju.[85]

The illegal fabrication and smuggling of guns reinforced organized crime considerably at the beginning of the 1990s. China became the first dealer of light guns on the American market in 1991, and more than 400 illegal manufacturers of firearms were shut down in the second half of 1994.[86] An internal document diffused by the Military Commission of the Central Committee[87] revealed that most of the guns deployed by drug trafficking and smuggling organizations were fabricated in China and came from either thefts or purchases, either from the Army and security forces, or from small private arsenals. Since 1990, 400 sentries have been killed in thefts from gun depots. The smuggling of state-of-the-art guns increased at the borders, and the counterfeit guns manufactured in illegal factories were of excellent quality. On top of this, gun manufacturers designated by the State often surpassed their authorized production, maximizing their profits and increasing the supply of illicit guns. The committed offences were planned in a spectacular manner,[88] even to the point of threatening the State Summits. In February 1996, the vice-president of the National Assembly, Li Peiyao, who was seen as the successor to the vice-president of the Republic, Rong Yiren, was assassinated by one of his own guards when he surprised him during a theft. This murder, which shook the Chinese government, was without doubt the reason for the 'punch against delinquency' (*yanda*) campaign. This explains the incredible increase in capital executions announced in the same year. During the Li Peiyao incident, the deputies expressed their dissatisfaction with regard to interior security by adopting, with 70 per cent of the votes – an insult, where unanimity is generally expected – the annual report of the President of the Popular Supreme Court. A statistic was circulating among party officials: more than 1550 officers were killed during the first half of the 1990s.[89]

In the social and ideological implosion context of the 1990s, the audacity of criminal organizations was essentially related to their firepower, as the Pingyuan incident shows. Situated in the southeast of Yunnan, in the Wenshan prefecture, near Vietnam, the region of Pingyuan has a population of 60 000 mountain people of *hui* Muslim minorities (8000 people), Zhuang and Miao. Many officials, such as the vice-chief of the district, Liu Hongen allowed the transformation of this territory into an independent kingdom, specialising in poppy farming, the manufacture of heroin and the counterfeiting of excellent quality American guns. An operation which mobilized more than 2000 police, army and special forces soldiers, was launched on 31 August 1992. It took three months of armed confrontation, and negotiation with the local godfather of drugs, called Ma Cilin, to pacify the district, resulting in the arrest of 854 traffickers, the seizure of 896 kilos of heroin and of important gun stocks, such as anti-tank grenades. This military operation was maintained under the utmost secrecy in order to prevent any collision with various minority populations, particularly the *hui* Muslims, who had developed drug trafficking toward Sichuan and the Chinese northwest.[90]

However, this locally focused operation did not decrease the smuggling of drugs and guns. In 1994, in the provinces of Yunnan and Guangxi, the border guards of the Public Security Ministry discovered 156 gun trafficking businesses related to drugs: the seizures no longer contained just original or counterfeit war guns, hand grenades, or anti-tank grenades, but a dozen bazookas, rocket launchers and heavy machine guns.[91] That same year, the government sent 8000 activists to the border regions of the Golden Triangle 'to encourage the masses to combat the use and the trafficking of drugs'.[92] The people of the border regions were thus far from being convinced of the harmful consequences of opiates.

Gun and drug smuggling today are gaining ground on the Chinese coasts: Guangxi, with its 1600 km of coasts, Guangdong, the Haïnan Island and Fujian, which have close links with the Hong Kong and Taiwan triads, Zhejiang and the region of Wenzhou, in the south of Shanghai, the peninsula of Shandong and the province of Liaoning, in Manchuria. Soft drugs are also involved: on 22 April 1994, a unit of coastal guards of Guangdong carried out the most important marijuana seizure since 1949 (1.4 tons), and arrested 15 traffickers.[93]

The shocking contrast between the highly repressive policy of the government and the arming of the criminal organizations emphasizes the importance that the drug question holds today and invites us to return to the original elements of these operations.

The expansion and diversification of drugs supplies

The first element concerns the expansion and diversification of drug supply, which essentially depends on Burmese heroin production as well as Chinese production. In fact, in just a few years, China went from being a transit country to being a drug producing country, to an extent that it is very difficult to evaluate. An interview with Chinese officials suggested that the poppy is illegally cultivated in 27 of the 30 Chinese provinces.[94] The poorest peripheral regions are those that are the most seriously affected, from the southeast (Yunnan, Sichuan, Guizhou, Guangxi) to the north of the country (Qinghai, Ningxia, Xinjiang, Gansu, Mongolia, Jilin and Heilongjiang in Manchuria), but other plantations have been discovered in Hunan, the province where Mao came from, in Hebei, not far from the capital, and even in the suburbs of Shanghai.[95]

As of 1990, poppies were grown in Sichuan, in the villages of the Maoxian district mountains, formerly a producer before 1949, and where a resurgence of opium abuse can be observed.[96] In 1991, poppy farming and drug trafficking reached 'dangerous proportions' in Qinghai, on the high plateau of Tibet, according to the vice-governor of the province.[97] During the same year, airborne inspections carried out by the forest police in the Daxing'anling Mountains, in Mongolia, revealed that hundreds of raw hectares were planted by poppy producers who sowed during the spring for an autumn harvest. Following a systematic discovery of the plantations by satellite, the forest guard units proceeded to destroy them by organizing fourteen aeroplane flights spreading weed-killer. Illicit farming covers 300 hectares, an area allowing the cultivation of three tons of opium or 300 kg of heroin, on the basis of an average productivity of 10 kg of opium per acre. Simultaneously, the forest police took out on the ground about 6 million poppies, with which 30 to 60 kg of opium could have been produced.[98] Mongolia therefore appears to be the principal producing region of drugs, judging by the destruction described above: during the first half of 1992, the *People's Daily* announced the seizure of 3 million poppies in the territory,[99] which corresponds to a potential harvest of 30 kilos of opium. Two years later, the *China Daily* implicitly recognizes the extension of illicit farming, in 'the contrasts between the rapid increase in consumption and the precariousness of revenues of certain sectors that led the peasants to lose the sense of their duty and to use criminal methods to satisfy wealth appetites'.[100]

'The wealth appetites' in question are in fact a euphemism. For the mountain people, who were forgotten and left out of the reforms, poppy farming constitutes the shortest, albeit the most dangerous, way to escape poverty. Since 1984, the inequality of trade terms between the cities and the villages has deepened the differential between the average incomes of the rural and the city people, which was established at the end of the 1990s to be in the ratio of 1 to 4, if we take into account the various subsidies from which the urban world benefits.[101] Added to this national average, there are important geographical disparities between the coastal, central and western provinces. The GDP per capita of Guizhou is a dozen times lower than that of the municipality of Shanghai. The enclave mountains of southwest China, inhabited by minorities or by *han* who live some way from the main trade routes, account for half of the 70 million peasants who live below the poverty threshold, with an annual income of less than 500 yuans (US$60).[102]

The arrests and seizures carried out during the campaign against drugs in 1994 confirm the tendencies of these marginalized populations to escape poverty by cultivating opium poppies, with the support, sometimes, of interested local authorities.[103] In June 1994, 13 people of the province of Shaanxi were condemned to death for 'the production and trafficking of drugs'.[104] Three years later, there were 241 cases of illicit poppy farming in one single district of the same province.[105] In June 1994, the dismantling of a production and trafficking network involving 17 kg of heroin, employing 51 people from the provinces of Xinjiang, Gansu and Shaanxi, along the Silk Road, suggests that there are important links with the Golden Crescent and Central Asia. The uncontrolled emigration of the Chinese and of national minorities is facilitated by the corruption of local administrations of the former USSR: there are probably today hundreds of thousands of Chinese in Kazakhstan, dozens in Khirgizstan and many millions – about 2.5 million – in Russia.[106] The effective headquarters of the Chinese Gulag, on the high plateau of Tibet, the province of Qinghai, has increasingly been affected by the production of drugs and drug abuse, which 'affect the social order and stability'.[107] Tibet, which had remained unaffected until the 1990s, has since been 'penetrated by the international drug cartels'.[108] Further to the North, marijuana and poppy are still cultivated in the remote regions of Xinjiang, which is 'constantly infiltrated by trafficking networks', according to the local media.[109] Squeezed between Mongolia and Gansu, the autonomous Republic of Ningxia, populated by Muslims, is the highest region for production and trafficking: between 1990 and 1995, more than 47 kg of heroin were seized, solely in the Yinnan prefecture.[110] The drug, selling for 300 yuan ($36) per gram, would also come from Yunnan, passing through the cities of Tongxin and Weizhou, which are the two centres of local trafficking, and are dominated by the *hui* (Muslims). In the neighbouring province of Gansu, where the poppy is cultivated for pharmaceutical use, part of the cultivation is diverted to feed the illicit market, according to local residents. The Muslim district of Guanghe, situated to the south of the capital, Lanzhou, is considered to be one of the places most affected by drug trafficking in China.[111]

The illegal farming of poppy has also developed along the Golden Triangle, on the Sino–Burmese and Sino–Vietnamese borders, to such an extent that the opium production of Yunnan would be close to that of Laos today, with 200 tons according to the Geopolitical Observatory of Drugs.[112] Although it is difficult to confirm the data, the extent of the poppy plantations along the Sino–Burmese border, so close to Yunnan, cannot be denied. Witnesses reported this until the end of the 1980s, a few metres from the Wanding border, on the Burma road. Further south, poppies are cultivated on a large scale in the region adjoining the autonomous Cangyuan district. With the same ethnic community living on both sides of the border, this production seems to have carried over into Chinese territory.[113]

The national production of illegal opium by-products seems to be quite limited. This is not the case for metamphetamines ('*ice*' or '*shabu*' in Chinese), the fabrication of which has become a speciality of the Hong Kong and Taiwan triads, with the intermediary help of mainland contacts. Since the 1980s, the traffickers have used the pharmaceutical and chemical enterprise services of various provinces under the cover of 'medicine'. This is how a chemical enterprise in Peking was able to deliver 479 kg of *ice* to dealers from Taiwan. Similar cases were discovered in Canton, in Xiamen (Amoy) and in Longmen in Fujian, where 310 kg of *ice* were seized on the production premises.[114] In 1991, the annual seizure of *ice* was 351 kg,[115] but this has increased considerably since then. On October 7 1994, attention was drawn to this trade when a number of Philippinos boarded two Chinese boats, the crew of which were in fact five soldiers from the People's Liberation Army. The boat's cargo amounted to 150 kg of '*shabu*'. A report from the Bangkok Interpol revealed that *ice* was produced in a Chinese military camp, under the control of a general who introduced 200 kg per cargo into the Philippines.[116] 1994 also saw the dismantling of another network of narcotics production in Fujian, destined for the Hong Kong and Taiwan gangs.[117] The manufacture of synthetic drugs or chemical precursors may easily be conducted on the Chinese territory, a consequence of the weak regulations and of the development of trade with the diaspora. From mid-1994 until the end of 1995, more than 40 tons of acetic anhydride, originating from China and destined for Pakistan via Hong Kong, the United Arab Emirates, Iran and Afghanistan, were seized.

From this point of view, the Middle Empire remained for a long time just as over-lenient as certain European countries: during the same period, more than 50 tons of acetic anhydride originating from Germany – in other words a sufficient quantity to produce 20–40 tons of heroin, were seized in Turkey.[118] Xinjiang occupies an important place in the trafficking of chemical precursors. It is an important producer of ephedrine, just as are Ningxia and Mongolia, and a zealous exporter of ephedrine destined for Pakistan, as witnessed by a seizure of 10 tons of this product at the end of 1997.[119] Despite these new developments, which contribute to the dynamism and diversification of the internal drugs supply, trafficking essentially continues to be fed by the massive smuggling of opium by-products in the neighbouring regions of the Golden Triangle. From this point of view, the drug revival in China must be set in the context of Sino-Burmese relations, as the latter emerge in Yunnan province.

Yunnan: Drugs and geopolitics in Sino–Burmese relations

Approximately one-third of the population of 38 million in Yunnan is composed of 'national minorities': the region includes 25 of the 55 ethnic groups which are spread across the whole of China. In addition, the province demonstrates significant economic backwardness, listing 75 of its districts among the 120 poorest in the country as a whole and having 10 per cent of its rural groups classed under the national poverty threshold (an annual per capita income of less than 500 yuan), that is 7 million in a population of 70 million.[120] Yunnan essentially consists of the minorities situated in the mountains along the 1897 kilometres of the border with Burma, an area inherited from the English colony of the nineteenth century. In 1886, the British seized Kokang, in the north of the Golden Triangle, where many Chinese had found refuge following the failure of the Muslim insurrection of Yunnan in the years 1850–60. In the 1960s, the Kokang was reattached to Burma as part of the agreement negotiated between Zhou Enlaï and Ne Win. History has thus passed down a border populated by a transnational mosaic. The same ethnic groups find themselves in both countries, in the north with the Kachins converted into Protestants (the 'Jingbos' of Yunnan), with the Sino–Burmese of Kokang, with the 'shan' Buddhists (the Chinese 'daï'), cousins of the Thai and of Laos, with the Karen Catholics or the Was, former headhunters. Further to the south, in the region of Xishuangbanna, we find Hanis, Lahus, Yis, Bulangs, Miaos, Yaos.[121] The densest part of the Golden Triangle corresponds to the Shan states of Burma, where the majority of the population is non-Shan: Lahus, Lisus and mainly Was; 'practically no road traced the thick jungle which covers the high mountains of two to three thousand metres, at the summit of which villages and local tribes are situated.'[122]

From 1970 to 1989, the Communist Party of Burma (CPB), a Peking satellite, controlled the majority of the Shan states, in open rebellion against the central power of Rangoon. Peking's aid started at the time of the state coup of General Ne Win, which overthrew the democratic government and did not ally with the Prime Minister, U Nu. In 1967, after the anti-Chinese riots in Rangoon and the evacuation of 100 000 people of Chinese origin, Mao increased his support for the CPB by dispatching massive military aid as well as many thousands of voluntary red guards, mostly originating from Yunnan, to become cadres of the CPB troops, who essentially came from the minorities of the mountain people. That same year, the CPB directors converted themselves into Mao supporters, with the sordid trial and execution of two of its leaders, Batin and Yebaw Htay, respectively described as 'the Burmese Deng Xiaoping and Liu Shaoqi.'[123] The death of Mao and the accession to power of Deng Xiaoping in 1978 marked a new political turn for Peking. China increased its close ties with Burma, recalled its volunteers, and considerably reduced its military and financial aid. It even offered comfortable retreats in Yunnan to Maoist ideologists of the CPB, on several occasions.

The financial difficulties of the CPB led to an increasingly frequent recourse to poppy farming and to heroin manufacturing, which were blocked by the leaders of the party during a prohibition campaign in 1985. Subsequently, the conflicts increased between the old Maoist leaders and the young local executives of the party, who were getting further involved in the production and trafficking of heroin in the majority of the war zones that they controlled, ultimately representing 80 per cent of the opium harvest in the Golden Triangle. In 1988, faced with the emergence of the Burmese Democratic Movement, the leaders of the CPB followed a non-interventionist line by following an old strategy of 'surrounding the cities by countryside.'

This policy favoured the resounding defeat of the urban opposition and the formation of the State Law and Order Revolutionary Committee (SLORC), which replaced the elected government on 18 September. The retreat of western aid and the diplomatic isolation of the dictatorship led the new leaders of Rangoon towards Peking, which developed its trade with Burma without sparing its support for the SLORC. Following the Tian'anmen massacres, the dictatorship's right-hand man, Khin Nyunt, responsible for information services, showed his sympathy towards China, which was experiencing 'similar disorders as Burma had in 1988'. The Sino–Burmese friendship has remained firm ever since. Peking signed arms and formation contracts for 1.2–1.4 billion dollars with Rangoon, reinforcing the military capacity of the Burmese junta, whose army increased from 190 000 to 300 000 men. Many delegations of the SLORC left for the Chinese capital or for Kunming. In December 1994, the official visit of Prime Minister Li Peng to Rangoon was designed to reaffirm these ties. Even if the Burmese junta has a tendency to diversify its arms purchase to include Russia,[124] China remains 'the most confident friend of the Myanmar people' according to the declarations made by the president of the SLORC, Than Shwe, during the last visit to Rangoon by Li Ruihuan, representing the Chinese People's Consultative Conference.[125]

The crucial moment of rapprochement between the two countries dates back to the break-up of the Burmese Communist Party, who controlled the principal opium production zones of the Shan states. On 12 March 1989, two local commandants of the Kokang regions, the brothers Peng Jiasheng and Peng Jiafu, invaded the general CPB district at Pangshang, before the border city of Wanding, on the road to Burma. The Was units refused to serve any longer as cannon fodder in the conflict between the CPB and the Burmese army, or its anti-Communist militia the Ka Kwe Ye (KKY), the latter recruited from the rebel underground which transferred its support to Rangoon and at the same time went into opium trafficking. They supported the rebellions that were significant to such an extent that, on April 17, the leaders of the CPB were forced to find refuge in China. We might then have expected an alliance between the rebels and the rebellious units of the Burmese Democratic Alliance (BDA), regrouping the diverse ethnic forces in rebellion against Rangoon and the thousands of students and villagers who took to the maquis after the crushing of the democratic movement in 1988. But the negotiations carried out with the mediation of the opium lord, Luo Xinghan, a Yunnanese installed at Lashio and former official of the local militia of KKY, allowed the situation to shift in favour of the military junta. Khin Nyunt slowly negotiated a cease-fire and agreements with the three principal military commandants controlling the zone of the former CPB in the Shan state, in exchange for an autonomous status which gives them the standing of a *de facto* prefecture, and the possibility of developing commercial activities without restriction. These agreements are the origin of the explosion of poppy farming and heroin manufacturing in Burma (Table 2.2).

In Kokang, the brothers Peng Jiasheng and Peng Jiafu were evicted by Yang Maoliang and Yang Mao'an, descendants of a royal family of 'sawbwa' Shan.

The Wa region is controlled in the North by Bao Youxiang and Li Ziru and in the central part by Chao Nilaï, all of them former military executives of the CPB. Further south, near Kengtung, the forces of Lin Mingxian and Zhang Zhiming (U Sailin and U Khy Myint in Burmese, two former red guards of Yunnan), both of whom have become first the challengers, then the successors, control the neighbouring regions of Xishuangbanna, by threatening the supply of opium of Khun Sa.[126] The new lords of the Golden Triangle share with their predecessors, Luo Xinghan and Khun Sa, dual Sino–Burmese nationality, but they are distinguished by their communist pasts which facilitate their contacts in China. They are regularly welcomed in Rangoon by Khin Nyunt, the leader of the dictatorship, to discuss regional

Table 2.2 The cultivation of poppy, the production and exportation of heroin in Burma 1987–1995

Years	Poppy cultivation (hectares)	Heroin production (tons)	Heroin exportation (tons)
1987	92300	53	51
1988	103200	68	66
1989	142742	128	123.5
1990	150100	180	174.5
1991	161012	185	181.5
1992	153700	180	174.5
1993	165800	190	186.5
1995		230	

Sources: US State Department. For 1995, US State Department, quoted in Radio Australia External Service, 28 December 1995, SWB BBC Asia-Pacific, 30 December 1995. From Chinese sources, the production of opium was estimated at about 2 500 tons in 1995: *China Daily*, 18 April 1995.

development programmes, alternative crops for cultivation or the expansion of tourism.[127]

Regularly attacked by Rangoon troops since 1993, erroneously believing him to control the majority of the heroin production of the Golden Triangle, Khun Sa served as a scapegoat and as a mediated cover for the profitable activities of his post-communist successors. Originating from a Chinese family who had lived in the North of Burma for more than two centuries, Khun Sa was able to become the 'king of opium' thanks to his merchant networks from the cultivation of villages controlled by the CPB, and due to his considerable firepower, and also as a result of the extent of financial corruption he utilized in Thailand, and his privileged relations with associates of Bangkok, Hong Kong and Taiwan who owned heroin refineries operating on his territory.[128] The Mong Tai Army, which he controlled from his HQ of Homong in the south of the Shan states, 30 km from the Thai border, numbered 15 000 men – the equivalent of the CPB troops in the 1980s – but they were better equipped than the communist guerrillas, with a heavier gun arsenal and SAM 7 ground–air missiles. Following the seizure by the Burmese army of the headquarters of the Karen from Manerplaw in January 1995, which served as a fallback option for the ethnic resistance and for the political opposition to dictatorship,[129] Khun Sa appears to have been the only pocket of resistance against SLORC power. In fact the 'opium king' was weakened by the gradual hemming-in of his territory, the reduction of his supplies, the dismantling of his intermediaries in Thailand and a rebellion by some of his troops, maybe 1000–6000 men, who blamed his 'Chinese businessmen for using the Shan independence cause, in order to hide their involvement in drug trafficking.'[130] In November 1995, Khun Sa announced his political withdrawal at the age of 60 and seems to have secretly negotiated his escape and the surrender of his headquarters with the Burmese junta, which was being peacefully used by the beginning of 1996. The surrounding of Khun Sa's HQ was carried out by the Burmese army with 3000 men from the Was units, greatly implicated in heroin production of the Golden Triangle. Rangoon is thus trying to cheaply regain regional and international recognition in order to facilitate its new international policy and the attraction of foreign capital.[131]

These great manoeuvres by SLORC hide their real purpose, which has been in place since 1989: the former red guards and officers of the CPB took Khun Sa's lead by reconverting themselves to trafficking narcotics. The only difference is that the new opium lords no longer have to hide in the jungle: taking advantage of cease-fire agreements and an official status in Rangoon, often using their dual nationality, they may freely invest their fortunes in legitimate businesses in Burma or in China. This financial power and political protection of the young generation explains the relative impunity of a trafficking organized on a grand scale, according to the declarations of Colonel Si Jiuyi, responsible for the Armed Police of Yunnan: the smuggling of 100–200 kg of opium by-products is becoming more frequent. The traffickers are inclined to be armed and to communicate via mobile telephones or walkie-talkies. The communities of the ethnic groups which populate the two sides of the Sino–Burmese border (1897 km), the Sino–Laotian border (700 km) and the Sino-Vietnamese border (1463 km) in particular make the work of the Armed Police more delicate.[132] In certain regions, the borders are not clear. The trafficking networks guarantee pensions for the families of smugglers who are arrested or executed. When caught, traffickers often make comments such as: 'You may kill me, but my descendants will take advantage,' or 'I may do time, but I'll remain rich for the rest of my life.' Certain traffickers even organize suicide commando groups: an explosive cargo is hidden under the stomach of a mule or a horse; if they see a likelihood of being captured by the police, the cargo is triggered, destroying the traffickers along with the guns and luggage.[133]

There are no general data on those who carry out the smuggling under the orders of the great traffickers, but some facts are available. The first striking detail is the over-representation of the *hui*, the Chinese Muslims, held under sentence of death following public trials organized across the province. This important Muslim minority of Yunnan was present at the Pingyuan incident, which set the police army troops against the traffickers. Drug smuggling still seems to be linked to the two former silk roads, the Central Asia land roads, and the maritime routes, which passed through Yunnan, Burma and the Indian Ocean. Some *ouighours* of Xinjiang are very active in the diffusion of narcotics-trafficking from Yunnan to the rest of the country. The important Muslim minority of Yunnan is also located on the other side of the border, where these Sino-Burmese, known as the 'Pathays', for many centuries led merchant caravans to the border of Burma, of Thailand and of Laos. Installed as businessmen in the Shan states, in Mandalay and in Rangoon, they are immediately distinguished as Burmese by their religion, and as Chinese by their ancestors.[134]

The second significant aspect is the predominance of youth in the drugs world: the 'hooked' (*yin junzi*) who 'climb to heaven' (*qu tianwang*) with the n°4 are identified as being between the ages of 15 and 40.[135] The third dimension, which mainly concerns the smuggling regions, is the predominance of the peasants: of a group of 28 traffickers condemned to death in an autonomous district of Yunnan in October 1991, 23 were peasants, two were municipal employees, two were farmers' sons and there was one single foreigner to the province who came from Peking. The fourth feature is the educational level of the small-time traffickers: in the same group of smugglers (23 men and 5 women), qualified as being 'very representative', six had completed primary school, nine had reached the first cycle of secondary school, and one had been to university.[136]

If there are no data concerning the ethnic affiliations of the people in question, in order not to revive the tensions between the *hans* and the minorities,[137] it is evident that the great traffickers of the Golden Triangle have used the services of the transnational people, who know the borders well, to pass the drug in small quantities. Despite the *Daï*, who represent the local lords and are used to working with the *hans*, the ethnic groups are very poor and massively illiterate: in Xishuangbanna, for example, two-thirds of the mountain people – except for the Jinuos – are illiterate, and more than half of the residents under 12 years of age do not know how to read.[138] Here as elsewhere, drug production and trafficking are the most attractive answers to social marginalization. The first consequence of the trafficking explosion and the consumption of heroin in Yunnan is that of the concomitant delinquency: in the entire province, we estimated that 40 per cent of arrests are related to drugs,[139] but at Kunming, this proportion reached 70 per cent, with a concomitant increase in rivalry between consumer–trafficker bands. Often subject to aggression, taxi drivers have been forced to install 'gates' to separate them from their clients.

The high price of heroin in Kunming, about 200 yuans per gram in 1994, in other words half an average monthly salary, pushes the 'hooked' to resell, stimulating the market and delinquency: we estimate that three-quarters of the n°4 followers commit a range of offences,[140] a proportion that is repeated at the national level. In the case of drug-addicted women, who are often initiated by their boyfriends, 90 per cent of them prostitute themselves to satisfy their drug needs, according to the same data covering the territory.[141] Research completed on 126 heroin addicts of Kunming revealed that 39 per cent practised prostitution before becoming drug-addicts, and 87 per cent afterwards.[142] By stigmatising drug users, and systematically branding them as delinquents, support was implicitly given to the repressive measures carried out by local police, customs services, Public Security forces and Interpol. In May 1995, the United Nations Drug Control Program (UNDCP) granted aid of US$2.9 million over three years, destined to reinforce the drug trafficking control capacity in Yunnan. A ministerial level meeting was held at the same time in Peking under the initiative of the UNDCP in order to co-ordinate the fight against drugs between China, Burma, Laos, Cambodia, Thailand and Vietnam.[143] The consumption of drugs is not only high in China, but also in Burma, which today has 300 000 heroin addicts on its territory, 70 per cent of whom are HIV-positive.[144]

The extension of trafficking between these two countries is clearly shown by the increasingly invasive Chinese presence in Burma, on a political, diplomatic and commercial level. For the Burmese dictatorship, isolated since 1988, China, after Tian'anmen, is seen as a model of international recognition of a despotic regime. Peking, as we have seen, has handled its military and diplomatic support in Rangoon by selling arms that are partially paid for by direct and indirect deductions carried out on heroin. As of 1988, the World Bank estimated that 40 per cent of the GDP of the Burmese economy, about US$3 billion, was fed by the smuggling of wood, jade, rubies, precious stones and heroin, which corresponds to its overall trade with China.[145] About 90 per cent of this is conducted as barter economy or compensation following the over-valuation of the Burmese rupee: the official exchange rate is 20–30 times higher than the market rate.[146] The US State department estimates a revenue of US$1.2 billion for heroin and opium exports in 1996, an amount that can be compared with official exports of US$891 million, and with the gross domestic product, estimated at US$107.5 billion at the official exchange rate and US$5.86 billion at the market rate.[147] In these conditions, the registered trade between China and Burma is only the tip of the iceberg, a useful footbridge for all sorts of trafficking. The vice-governor of Yunnan declared in April 1995 that 50 tons of Burmese heroin were exported annually via its province, a figure which corresponds with the most cautious estimations of Chinese consumption (40 tons).[148]

Yunnan's free trade with its Burmese neighbour, as well as with Laos and Vietnam, is a general strategy that aims to correct the great disparities accumulated under the leadership of Deng Xiaoping between the coastal regions and the interior regions, all by developing the full-scale border trade.[149] About 90 per cent of the trade between these two countries transits through the prefecture of Dehong, situated on the former road to Burma, rebuilt today in the Chinese zone. The two principal border posts, Wanding-Panghsai and Ruili-Muse, have developed considerably with a trade of over US$15 million in 1984 increasing to US$800 million in 1994, in other words an important part of the foreign trade of the province.[150] Burma represents 80 per cent of the border commerce of Yunnan, the rest being sent to Vietnam and some to Laos, where the Chinese from Yunnan control the economy of border cities.[151] The terms of trade are essentially favourable to the Chinese, who import jade, wood, rubber and other agricultural products (rice, shrimp), and export motorized tractors, textiles and consumer goods (gas lamps, televisions, hi-fi). This explains the considerable increase in the foreign commerce of the province which reached, in 1995, US$1.3 billion solely from imports.[152] This trade allowed border districts to escape from poverty and to close the gap between themselves and other rural districts of the province.[153]

For the Burmese, the trade with Yunnan represented 40 per cent of their foreign commerce. Just because of their very low prices, Chinese consumer products, from electrical appliances to bicycles, have a tendency to invade the markets of Mandalay and Lashio, substituting for the local products or for products smuggled from Thailand.[154] To this 'invasion' of Chinese products, which even the Vietnamese complain about, is added the presence of Yunnan businessmen who take advantage of false papers, and the presence of Sino–Burmese from Kokang, who monopolize the market for massive investments in hotel trade and real estate.[155] In a very significant article, *Newsweek* magazine even asked whether Mandalay was about to become the next Chinese province: the Chinese multiplied their commercial businesses there during the 1990s, and 800 000 tourists from the Middle Empire visited Burma in 1994. Most of them are businessmen who made their fortunes by buying rice, gold, wood and precious stones, and by reselling consumer products to Burma at very good prices. The trafficking of false identity cards, purchasable for a few hundred dollars, has developed. With a Burmese death in the province, newcomers from Yunnan or elsewhere are 'reincarnated'.[156]

The question that immediately comes to mind is the relationship between the legal and illegal commerce. The considerable natural resources of Burma have allowed a rent-seeking economy to develop in the context of liberalization of trade under the control of the junta. The commercial deficit continued to grow from 1991 to 1996, from US$469 million to more than US$1 billion, according to the IMF. The purchase of consumer goods, superior to equipment goods, represents more than 40 per cent of imports.[157] The current account deficit goes up to US$300 million, in other words 6 per cent of GDP evaluated at the market rate, and the foreign debt stands at US$1.5 billion. As well as Japanese aid, which allows the servicing of the loan debt, deficits are reduced by tourism receipts but mainly by recycling the profits of the smuggling commerce, which feeds important private transfers (about US$1.5 billion from 1991 to 1996) and a non-negligible part of direct foreign investments (US$931 million during the same period).[158] More than 70 per cent of effective investments are concentrated in petroleum and natural gas, mainly with the exploitation of the Yanada offshore oil-field, in the Martaban gulf, under the aegis of the French group, Total. But contrary to what has been underlined by the press, which tends to concentrate on investment promises, the Americans are also present, with 23 per cent of foreign investment stocks, ahead of the French (18 per cent) and the Singaporeans (11 per cent).[159] The hotel business, tourism and real estate are in the next most significant positions for foreign investments in Burma, together accounting for 23 per cent of the total stock.

These weakly profitable investments, given that numerous hotels stay empty, are often used to launder profits from narcotics. Bao Youxiang, chief of the United Wa State Army, in the Golden Triangle, thus recently acquired a part of an office tower in the centre of Rangoon. Khun Sa invested in bus companies and real estate business, whereas Luo Xinghan, his former rival, celebrated the marriage of his son, who succeeded him in the business, accompanied by eight ministers of SLORC.[160] Luo Xinghan used *Myanmar Fund* to recycle his narco-products, with the support of the *Government of Singapore Investment Corporation*, whose director, Eddie Taw Cheng Kong, was condemned to nine years in prison in May 1997.[161] The hard core of the *Myanmar Fund* shareholders, in which the American Bank Morgan Guaranty Trust Co. participates, is built by the *Government of Singapore Investment Corporation*. The former prime minister Lee Kuan Yew and many notable Singaporeans were known associates of the management of this fund.[162] An interesting detail reveals that the *Myanmar Fund*, quoted on the Dublin stock market, is a creation of the Sino-Malaysian billionaire Robert Kuok, one of the principal tycoons from Hong Kong, owner of the chain of Shangri-la hotels and of the *South China Morning Post*, the best English language daily newspaper in the former British colony.

Following a news report published by an Australian National Channel, the Prime Minister Goh Chok Tong denied the existence of all relations between the Singapore government and the drug traffickers, by accusing the opposition of having become disloyal towards its country, and of tarnishing its reputation with foreigners.[163] If the city-state is proving itself to be exceptionally severe towards heroin traffickers, condemning dozens of people to death annually, the question of its role in the recycling of the Burmese drug money remains unanswered.

The local reinvestment of narco-profits was facilitated as of 1993 by governmental measures authorizing the Burmese to convert the foreign currency that they repatriated at a market rate, 20–30 times higher than the official exchange rate. The drug money, which was usually placed in Thailand or in China, thereafter fed the development of numerous hotels, bars, real estate societies, transport societies, all involved with traffickers.[164] One of the most crucial aspects of the foreign presence in Burma is the concentration of financial establishments, which cannot be explained with regard to the development level of the country. There are at least 70 financial institutions, 43 of which are foreign banks. Their activity is closely related to the recycling of illegal commercial profits, which surpass, as we have seen, official commercial levels.[165] A retired Burmese banker estimates that 'at least 60 per cent of the private business in Rangoon is related to drugs.'[166]

Illegal business has developed considerably during the 1990s: in 1992, the province of Yunnan reported 900 serious smuggling incidents, as many as the coastal province of Fujian, near Taiwan; in other words a twofold increase on the cases of the preceding year.[167] In the Kachins states, the smuggling essentially involves precious stones, the 'red line' of the ruby, and in the Shan States, the 'white line' of heroin. The rigidity of the Burmese exchange rate pushed 2400 Chinese

State enterprises, collective or private, which are engaged in the border trade, to take advantage of the compensation formulas which devote themselves to trafficking. The narco-profits are reconverted by the Sino–Burmese on both sides of the border. The loop is then closed, sealing the relations between the legal and illegal commerce, and the mobility they entail.

For Yunnan, as for southwestern China, and mainly the great province of Sichuan, access to Burma constitutes an important step towards the conquest of the emerging markets of southeast Asia, which already represent 30 per cent of the province's exports.[168] The longer-term objective may be to collaborate with Thailand, Burma, Laos, Cambodia and Vietnam, in order to allow 500-ton boats to navigate the Mekong, which would reduce the transport distance to southeast Asia by 2000 km, cutting 84 per cent off the time spent and 60 per cent off the costs.[169] But before realizing this complex transnational project, China aims to use its excellent relationship with the Burmese dictatorship to reopen the southwestern silk road, and to ensure privileged access to the Indian Ocean. As underlined by Bertil Lintner, the Peking projects have been worked on since as early as 1985 by the former communications vice-minister Pan Qi, who outlined the potential advantage of the reopening of the Kunmin–Ruili–Lashio–Indian Ocean axis, with regard to the Chinese exports and the disenclavement of the southwestern provinces.[170] The Chinese carried out the first step of this programme by reconstructing the Burma road, from Kunming to Ruili, in 1995. They offered their credit and services for the repair of the Ruili–Muse–Lashio section, particularly hazardous during the rainy season from October to March, and for the construction of a road from Daluo to Kengtung, destined eventually to extend to Chieng Mai in Thailand. During the negotiations that led to the final agreement, the Burmese party confirmed, according to official Chinese sources, 'that Yunnan may use Burma as an access road to the sea.'[171]

These purely civil agreements with Burma have been followed by Sino–Burmese co-operation on maritime information in the Coco Islands of the Indian Ocean, discovered at the end of 1992 by Western spy satellite. The Indian fleet's chief, Admiral V.S. Shekawat, visited Peking in the spring of 1996, which itself is a sign of these developments. Indian marine officials were kept informed of the Sino–Burmese co-operation, which has led to 'radar and telescope installations not far from the Andamans Islands,' attached to the Union territory. The Chinese also proceeded, according to the same sources, with hydraulic layouts around the Coco and Hainggyi Islands. Three Chinese trawlers with sophisticated equipment were apprehended in questionable circumstances, while they navigated in the Indian territorial waters of the Andaman sea in August 1994. China also promised to train officers in the Burmese navy and information services.[172] Peking even negotiated an installation in the Ramree Islands, on a line with the Arakan State, and at Victory Point, the most southerly island in the Burmese territory, not far from the Malacca strait. Despite the vigorous denials of Li Peng, during his visit to Rangoon in December 1994, these developments were closely followed by Japan, India and the ASEAN countries,[173] who were worried about potential relations with the new Chinese economic power, the affirmation of China's nationalist rhetoric, and the natural tendency of a large country such as China to transform its small neighbours into dependencies.

Some Burmese estimate today that the Chinese have accomplished through peaceful and subtle means what they were never able to obtain by supporting the CPB for a number of years.[174] Faced with this situation, Rangoon's attitude remains ambivalent. By displaying an independent will and the diversification of its commercial partners – consistent with its desire to integrate into ASEAN and to reintegrate the international community – the military junta would have been able to place new arms orders, for US$400 million during Li Peng's last trip: 20 gun helicopters,

50 artillery machines, 60 auto-machine guns and six patrols, according to the Bangkok press.[175] According to the same sources, Rangoon would even have proposed to Peking the setting up of joint ventures in arms supply for its defence and export needs.

These negotiations show very well the ambivalence of the Chinese policy, and more generally the positions that the States are often led to take in drug trafficking matters. The discrepancy between the currency reserves declared by Burma (US$300–350 million) and the real reserves placed in foreign banks, is equivalent to one or even three times if we choose to agree with 1992 evaluations. Numerous observers in Rangoon suspect that the narco-profits were used to finance the preceding arms purchases from China, which increased to more than US$ one billion.[176] During the press conference in Rangoon, Li Peng was pleased with the recent collaboration of Burmese authorities with regard to the fight against drugs, and expressed a wish that the two countries work together with United Nations agencies.[177] He knew all along, however, that the Chinese arms purchases were in part paid for by narco-profits, and that the new drug barons, former CPB or Sino–Burmese red guards, took advantage of an official statute that guaranteed to protect them from prosecution.

The same logic prevails when France sells its Mirage jets to Pakistan, aware that they are part financed by heroin trafficking; or when German companies export small amounts of the chemical precursors of heroin everywhere around the world accumulating to a massive amount in total. Over and above the simplistic accusations of 'the prevailing hypocrisy', this contradiction between the economic order and the legal order should lead us to question ourselves on the socio-economic stakes of drug trafficking, from both local and international points of view.

Notes

1 Cf. Michel Koutouzis, 'Drogues à l'Est: logique de guerre et de marché', *Politique Etrangère*, Spring 1995, no. 1.
2 Cf. *International Herald Tribune*, 3 May 1995.
3 Cf. Dusan T. Batakovic, 'Les magnats rouges en Europe du sud-est: l'économie, la politique et la mafia', *Rapport moral sur l'argent dans le monde*, Paris, Financial Economic Association, 1995, pp. 81–6.
4 Cf. Jack F. Matlock, 'Russia: the power of the mob', *The New York Review of Books*, 13 July, 1995; Stephen Handelman, *Comrade Criminal: Russia's New Mafia*, Yale University Press, 1995, p. 398. On the level of drug trafficking: cf. Elizabeth Joyce, 'New drugs, new responses: lessons from Europe', *Current History*, April 1998, p. 185.
5 Cf. *Lettre de Russie* no. 22, January 1995, Center for Research on Enterprises and Societies.
6 Matlock, 'Russia: the power of the mob'.
7 Cf. Esther Duflo, *Le Monde*, 6 September 1994.
8 Cf. *International Herald Tribune*, 21 February 1994.
9 Matlock, 'Russia: the power of the mob', p. 14.
10 Cf. Brigitte Breuillac, *La Tribune Desfossés*, 13 September 1994.
11 Handelman, *Comrade Criminal*.
12 Cf. Marie Laurence Guy, 'La criminalité organizée tous azimuts: l'exemple de la Russie', *Relations internationales et stratégiques*, no. 20, Winter 1995.
13 Cf. Rensselaer W. Lee III, 'Global Reach: the threat of international drug trafficking', *Current History*, May 1995, p. 215.
14 Cf. *Le Monde*, 22 October 1994 and the interview with Pavel Gratchev on the assassination of Dimitri Kholodov, *Izvestia* in *Lettre de Russie* no. 20, November 1994, Center for Research on Enterprises and Societies, Geneva.
15 Cf. Dimitri de Kochko and Alexandre Daskevitch, *L'empire de la drogue: la Russie et ses marchés*, Hachette 1994; Rensselaer W. Lee, III and Scott B. Mac Donald, 'Drugs in the East', *Foreign Policy* no. 90, Spring 1993, Washington; Michel Koutouzis, 'Drogues à l'Est: logiques de guerres et de marché', *Politique étrangère*, 1995, no. 1; Marc Galeotti, *Jane's Intelligence Review*, October 1994; *Moscow news*, 4–10 November, 1994.
16 Lee and Mac Donald, 'Drugs in the East'.
17 Michael Specter, 'A caravan of drugs crosses wilds of Central Asia', *International Herald Tribune*, 3 May 1995.
18 Cf. Jennifer G. Mathers, 'Corruption in the Russian armed forces', *The World Today*, August–September 1995.

19 Cf. Pierre Kopp (ed.), *L'économie du blanchiment*, Association d'économie financière, Caisse des dépots et consignations, Paris, 1995, p. 184.

20 Cf. Umberto Santino, in Alain Labrousse and Alain Wallon, *La planète des drogues*, Editions du Seuil, Paris, 1992. Thomas Schnee, *Le Monde diplomatique*, April 1994.

21 We cite here the American estimates of the US State Department, deduced from satellite observations and a supposed efficiency in hectares. Cf. 1995 report of the Geopolitical Observatory of Drugs, Editions du Seuil, 1995.

22 News report 'China white', *Time*, 6 January 1992.

23 Cf. *Beijing review*, 22–28 July 1992, pp. 16–18; *Beijing Information*, 2 January 1995; Dali L. Yang, 'Illegal drugs, policy change, and state power: the case of contemporary China', *The Journal of Contemporary China*, no. 4, Fall 1993.

24 Cf. *China Daily*, 1 April 1994 and *Summary of World Broadcasts, BBB, Asia Pacific*, shortly after SWB, 28 February 1995.

25 Cf. *Beijing Information*, 2 January 1995.

26 Cf. *China Daily*, 23 June 1995.

27 Cf. *China Daily*, 30 October 1995.

28 Cf. Zhonguo xinwen she, 27 July 1996, in SWB BBC Far East, 6 July 1996.

29 Cf. *China Daily*, 23 July 1997 and 30 July 1997.

30 Cf. *Nongmin ribao* (Quotidien des paysans), 6 May 1997, p. 2; *Renmin gong'an bao* (Journal of Public Security), 8 June 1997, p. 4; *Renmin zhengxie bao* (Journal of the Consultative Popular Assembly), 16 April 1997; in *China News Analysis*, 15 September 1997: 'The new opium war'.

31 Cf. Zhongguo xinwen she, 27 April 1997 in SWB BBC Asia Pacific, 29 April 97.

32 Cf. Yu Xiaodong and Li Yundong (Direction), *Da jin du* (The prohibition of drugs), Beijing, Tuanjie chubanshe, 1993, p. 64.

33 Ibid., p. 29.

34 Ibid., p. 364.

35 Ibid., p. 110 and p. 89.

36 Ibid., p. 359.

37 Ibid., p. 218.

38 Cf. Hua Lianwen, 'Guangdong xidu fandu xiezhen' (Review on drug trafficking and abuse in Guangdong), *Jiushi niandaï* (The nineties) no. 264, January 1992, p. 50, quoted in Dali L. Yang, 'Illegal drugs, policy change and state power: the case of contemporary China', *The Journal of Contemporary China*, no. 4, Fall 1993.

39 Cf. Pierre Kopp, 'L'efficacité des politiques de contrôle des drogues illégales', *Futuribles*, March 1994.

40 Cf. *China Daily*, 1 April 1994.

41 Dali L. Yang, 'Illegal drugs', p. 17.

42 Ibid., p. 18.

43 Cf. Li Jianhua et al., 'Community-based approaches to drug abuse demand reduction', Yunnan Institute of drug abuse, ESCAP United Nations, 1993, pp. 3–4.

44 Cf. Sun Jie, *Jinri redian jishi* (Chronical of the major points today), Changchun, Shidaï wenyi chubanshe, 1992, pp. 48–9, quoted in Dali L. Yang, 'Illegal Drugs', p. 16.

45 Cf. 'Asia's drug war', *The Wall Street Journal Europe*, 11 January 1995.

46 Cf. Alain Labrousse (ed.), *Atlas des drogues*, Geopolitical Drug Observatory, 1995.

47 Cf. Huang Wei, 'The increase of the fight against drugs', *Beijing Information*, 2 September 1996, p. 19.

48 Cf. *Renmin gong an bao* (Journal of Popular Security), 24 May 1997, p. 4, in *China News Analysis*, 15 September 1997.

49 Cf. Robert S. Gelbard, US Assistant Secretary of State, *Far Eastern Economic Review*, 21 November 1996.

50 Cf. 'Asia's drug war', *The Wall Street Journal Europe*, 11 January 1995.

51 Cf. Rapport du GAFI, *La lutte contre le blanchiment de capitaux*, La Documentation Française, 1990.

52 Dali L. Yang, 'Illegal Drugs', p. 18.

53 Cf. the declaration of the United Nations coordinator in *China Daily*, 10 January 1998.

54 Cf. Xinhua, 1 December 1996 in SWB BBC, 4 December 1996; *China news analysis*, no. 1562, 15 June 1996, pp. 2 and 5.

55 Dali L. Yang, 'Illegal Drugs', p. 19.

56 Cf. Zhu Entao, *China Daily*, 28 March 1995.

57 Cf. the seizure of 2.5 kg of heroin in Urumqui, the capital of Xinjiang and the arrest of five traffickers, two of whom were Pakistani, in *Summary of World Broadcasts, BBC Asia Pacific*, 5 December 1995.

58 Cf. AFP Peking, 27 March, 28 March and 2 April 1997.

59 An agreement on anti-drug co-operation was signed with the Russian Minister of Justice (cf. AFP Peking, 26 November 1996) and with the Mexican government, (AFP Peking, 22 and 24 November 1996).

60 Dali L. Yang, 'Illegal Drugs', p. 26.

61 Ibid., p. 26; *Time* magazine, 6 January 1992; Zhongguo xinwenshe, 21 March 1994; *China Daily*, 25 February 1995; *Jingji cankao* (economic references), 15 February 1995.

62 Cf. SWB BBC Asia Pacific, 29 July 1994.
63 Cf. *Beijing Information*, 11 December 1995, p. 15.
64 Cf. Zhou Feng, General secretary of the Narcotics Control Commission, in AFP, 25 June 1994.
65 Cf. AFP, 26 June 1994 and SWB BBC Asia Pacific, 4 July 1994.
66 Cf. Zhongguo xinwenshe, in SWB BBC Asia Pacific, 2 February 1995.
67 Cf. *China Daily*, 27 April 1995 and SWB BBC Asia Pacific, 3 June 1995.
68 Cf. SWB BBC Asia Pacific, 15 August 1995 and 3 June 1995; AFP, 25 June 1995.
69 Cf. Radio Guangdong, in SWB BBC Asia Pacific, 3 June 1995.
70 Cf. In 1996 alone, the Shenzhen services discovered 426 drug trafficking businesses, arrested 642 people and seized 647 kg of heroin; cf. *Beijing Information*, 19 May 1997.
71 Cf. Geopolitical Observatory on drugs, *La dépêche internationale des drogues* no. 57, July 1996.
72 Cf. AFP, 27 June 1996, and Jorge Svartzman, AFP, 17 July 1996. *Yangcheng wanbao*, Canton, 26 June 1996, p. 1 and *Gansu ribao*, Lanzhou, 27 June 1996, p. 1 reproduced in SWB BBC Far East, 15 July 1996.
73 Dali L. Yang, 'Illegal Drugs', p. 28, note 87.
74 Cf. *Far Eastern Economic Review*, 4 July 1996, p. 22.
75 Cf. AFP Peking, 25 August 1997.
76 Cf. Michael Dutton, 'The basic character of crime in contemporary China', *The China Quarterly*, no. 149, March 1997, p. 168.
77 Cf. Tao Yuan, 'Yunnan records progress in fighting drug dealers', *China daily*, 25 February 1995.
78 Cf. Xinhua, 7 October 1994; *Jingji cankao* (economical references), 15 February 1995; *China Daily*, 25 February 1995. *Jane's Intelligence Review*, special report no. 5, April 1995, p. 15.
79 Cf. *China Daily*, 18 April 1995.
80 Cf. *China Daily*, 4 June 1997.
81 Cf. *China Daily*, 20 June 1997.
82 Cf. *China Daily*, 23 June 1995. The number of rehabilitation centres changed from 251 to 500, according to Zhongguo xinwen she, 4 July 1996, in SWB BBC Far East, 10 July 1996.
83 Cf. Xinhua, 24 December 1996, in SWB BBC Asia Pacific, 1 January 1997.
84 Cf. *China Daily*, 22 November 1994.
85 Cf. *China Daily*, 28 March 1995 and Zhongguo tongxunshe, 7 March 1995 in SWB/BBC Asia Pacific, 25 March 1995.
86 Cf. Gordon White, 'Chinese socialism and its transition', *Chinese Social Sciences Quarterly* no. 5, November 1993, Hong Kong; AFP, 21 October 1994.

87 Cf. Mensuel *Zhengming* (The debate), Hong Kong, 1 September 1993, pp. 27–9.

88 Cf. *Mingbao*, Hong Kong, 29 May 1996, in SWB BBC Far East, 4 June 1996.

89 Cf. *Far Eastern Economic Review*, 4 July 1996, pp. 24.

90 Cf. *Nanfang ribao* (Southern Daily) in SWB/BBC Asia Pacific, 10 December 1992; SWB/BBC Asia Pacific, 28 January 1993; Dali Yang, 'Illegal Drugs'.

91 Cf. *Fazhi ribao* (The Law Daily), 23 February 1995, p. 3. Yunnan and Guangxi are the two provinces most hit by gun smuggling, frequently linked to drugs: cf. *Mingbao*, Hong Kong, 29 May 1996, in SWB BBC Far East, 4 June 1996.

92 Cf. *Zhongguo xinwenshe*, 13 September 1994 in SWB/BBC Asia Pacific, 14 October 1994.

93 Cf. *Quotidien du peuple*, 7 January 1995 in SWB/BBC Asia Pacific, 13 January 1995. On Zhejiang and the traffic in Wenzhou, cf. also *China Daily*, 12 October 1995. On the penetration of triads from Hong Kong in People's China, cf. also *China Daily*, 24 April 1995.

94 Cf. Nick Driver, 'Internal propaganda film underlines China drug fears', United Press International, 12 July 1992, quoted in Dali L. Yang, 'Illegal drugs'.

95 Dali L. Yang, 'Illegal Drugs', p. 20. On the persistence of the phenomena in 1995, see the declarations of the Public Security Director of Shanghaï, in SWB BBC Asia-Pacific, 10 July 1995, G/9. The problem started in 1997, when 10 000 poppy plants, spread between 80 producers, were once again destroyed in the Island of Chongming, which depends on the municipality of Shanghaï. Cf. Zhongguo xinwenshe, 19 May 1997 in SWB BBC, 21 May 1997. On the maintenance of marijuana and opium plantations in Xinjiang, cf. Television Xinjiang, 5 January 1996, in SWB BBC, 8 January 1996. For Qinghaï, cf. *Qinghaï ribao*, in SWB BBC, 3 May 1997.

96 Cf. *Quotidien du Sichuan*, 12 November 1990, quoted in Yu Xiaodong and Li Yundong, *Da jin du*, p. 223.

97 Cf. Radio Qinghaï, in SWB/BBC Far East, 18 January 1991.

98 Yu Xiaodong and Li Yundong, *Da jin du*, pp. 223–224.

99 Cf. *Quotidien du peuple*, 26 June 1992, quoted in SWB/BBC Far East, 16 July 1992.

100 Cf. *China Daily*, 3 May 1994.

101 Cf. Guilhem Fabre, article 'la Chine' in *Le monde des villes*, under the tutelage of Thierry Paquot, Editions Complexe, Brussels, 1996.

102 Cf. *China News Analysis*, 1 October 1995; *China Daily*, 1 July 1994 and 31 October 1995. For a discussion on the great poverty in China, greatly under-estimated in the official statistics, see

Guilhem Fabre, 'Voyage au centre du Guizhou', *Le Monde diplomatique*, May 1997.

103 Cf. *China Daily*, 23 April 1997, p. 2; Xinhua, 21 April 1997.

104 Cf. Xinhua news agency in SWB/BBC Asia-Pacific, 27 June 1994.

105 Cf. Shaanxi ribao (The Shaanxi daily), 16 July 1997, p. 7, in SWB BBC, 28 June 1997.

106 Cf. Firouzeh Nahavandi, 'The transitional difficulties towards democracy in Kazakhstan', *Transitions* Review, Université Libre de Bruxelles, 1994 no. 2, p. 105; Caroline Puel, *Le Point*, 1995.

107 Cf. Radio Qinghaï, SWB BBC Asia Pacific, 2 July 1994.

108 Cf. Xinhua, 26 June 1997 in SWB BBC, 28 June 1997, and Tibet Television, in SWB BBC, 14 December 1996.

109 Cf. *Xinjiang ribao*, 5 June 1996, p. 1, in SWB BBC Far East, 28 June 1996.

110 Cf. *Ningxia ribao* (The Ningxia Daily), 20 October 1995 in SWB BBC Asia Pacific, 6 December 1995.

111 Cf. Gilles Campion, AFP, 18 July 1996.

112 Cf. *Géopolitique des drogues*, Paris, 1995, OGD. On the case of illegal poppy farming in the borders of Yunnan, see Zhongguo xinwenshe in SWB BBC Asia Pacific, 7 July 1994 and 20 January 1995.

113 Cf. *Jingji cankao* (economical references), 15 February 1995.

114 Dali L. Yang, 'Illegal Drugs', pp. 21–2.

115 Cf. *Quotidien du peuple*, in SWB BBC Asia-Pacific, 4 April 1992.

116 Cf. *Géopolitique des drogues*, Paris, OGD, 1995.

117 Cf. Agence Xinhua, in SWB BBC Asia-Pacific, 27 June 1994.

118 Cf. Report of the OIC in 1995, Vienna, 1996, p. 27.

119 Cf. Zhonguo xinwen she, 12 November 1997 in SWB BBC, 15 November 1997.

120 Cf. *China Daily*, 4 September 1995; 19 December 1994.

121 For a general presentation of Xishuangbanna, cf. Wu Zhaolu and Ou Xiaokun, *The Xishuangbanna Biosphere Reserve: A Tropical Land of Natural and Cultural Diversity*, UNESCO Man and Biosphere Program Working Paper, 1995.

122 Cf. Catherine Lamour and M.R. Lamberti, *Les grandes manoeuvres de l'opium*, Paris, Point-Seuil, p. 171.

123 Cf. Martin Smith, *Burma, Insurgency and the Politics of Ethnicity*, p. 233; Bertil Lintner, *The Rise and Fall of the CPB*, Cornell University Press, 1990.

124 Cf. *Financial Times*, 14 November 1995.

125 Cf. *China Daily*, 12 December 1995.

126 Cf. Bertil Lintner, *Burma in Revolt, Opium and Insurgency Since 1948*, ch. 8, Westview Press, Boulder, 1994; Bertil Lintner, *Jane's*

Intelligence Review, February 1994, and special report no. 5, April 1995.

127 Cf. T.V. Myanmar, Rangoun, 17 June 1995, on the interview with Khin Nyunt, U Saï Lin (alias Lin Mingxian) and U Kyi Myint (alias Zhang Zhimin) in SWB, BBC Far East, 22 June 1995.

128 Cf. Bertil Lintner, *Burma in Revolt*, p. 254.

129 Cf. André and Louis Boucaud, *Le Monde diplomatique*, May 1995.

130 Cf. *Far Eastern Economic Review*, 9 March 1995 and 19 October 1995.

131 Cf. Jean Claude Pomonti, *Le Monde*, 4 and 7–8 January 1996.

132 Cf. Zhongguo xinwenshe, 21 March 1994 quoted in SWB BBC Asia Pacific, 16 December 1994.

133 Cf. The *Dengdaï* Review, Hong Kong, 15 November 1994, pp. 68–9, in SWB BBC Asia-Pacific, 16 December 1994.

134 Cf. 'The SLORC and Islam', *The Sunday Post*, Bangkok, 4 September, 1994.

135 Yu Xiaodong and Li Yundong, *Da jin du*, p. 362.

136 Ibid., p. 230.

137 On these tensions, see Jin Yen in *Zhengming* (The debate), Hong Kong, May 1994, pp. 39–41.

138 Wu Zhaolu and Ou Xiaokun *The Xishuangbanna biosphere reserve*, p. 43.

139 Yu Xiaodong and Li Yundong, *Da jin du*, p. 363.

140 Ibid.

141 Cf. 'Tzu Ching', Hong Kong, 5 December 1995 in SWB BBC Asia-Pacific, 5 January 1996.

142 Cf. Li Jianhua *et al.*, 'Community-based approaches to drug abuse demand reduction', 1993, Yunnan Institute of Drug Abuse.

143 Cf. Xinhua, 26 May 1995, in SWB BBC Asia-Pacific, 29 May 1995; *China Daily*, 23 May 1995.

144 Cf. Radio Australia, 28 December 1995, in SWB BBC, 30 December 1995; *Far Eastern Economic Review*, 21 November 1996, p. 35.

145 Cf. Martin Smith, *Burma: Insurgency and the Politics of Ethnicity*, p. 25.

146 Cf. IMF: Myanmar: Recent Economic Developments, April 1997.

147 Ibid., p. 14.

148 André and Louis Boucaud, *Le Monde diplomatique*, May 1996.

149 Cf. 'China's blueprint for border trade development', *China Economic News*, 15 August 1994; Teh-chang Lin, 'The development of China's border trade', *Issues and Studies*, July 1996.

150 Cf. *Da gongbao*, Hong Kong, 21 December 1994, in SWB BBC, 22 December 1994; *China Daily*, 15 July 1995, p. 10. The Burmese data are nevertheless much lower: their figure for 1995–96 is a

border commercial total of US$273 million, 176 of which are with China (24 for exportation and 152 for importation). Cf. IMF, Myanmar: Recent Economic Development, 1997. The data for Yunnan for 1996 are also more modest: US$362 million for the commerce with Thailand, Vietnam and Laos. Cf. *Far Eastern Economic Review*, 11 September 1997, p. 55. Xinhua, 4 May 1997 in SWB BBC Asia-Pacific, 6 May 1997.

151 Cf. Florence Rossetti, 'La renaissance du fait chinois au Laos', *Perspectives chinoises*, July–August 1997, p. 29.
152 Cf. SWB BBC Asia-Pacific, 19 June 1996.
153 Cf. Guangzhi Zhao, 'A model of decentralized development: border trade and economic development in Yunnan', *Issues and Studies*, October 1996.
154 Cf. Christian Lechervy and Collignon, manuscript article on Burma, p. 29. The Burmese data presented to the IMF are very different: China represents only 5 per cent of exportation and 12 per cent Burmese importations, far behind Singapore. Cf. IMF, Myanmar: Recent economic developments, 1997.
155 Cf. *Far Eastern Economic Review*, 16 February 1995.
156 Cf. *Newsweek*, 19 June 1995, p. 5 and *Far Eastern Economic Review*, 22 December 1994, p. 26.
157 Cf. IMF, Myanmar: Recent Economic Developments, April 1997, pp. 30 and 101.
158 Ibid., p. 108.
159 Ibid., p. 110.
160 Cf. Guy Lubeigt, 'La société birmane face à la question institutionnelle', *Revue d'études comparatives est–ouest*, no. 3, Septembre 1997, p. 173; Robert Gelbard, United States' assistant secretary of state, *Far Eastern Economic Review*, 21 November 1996; *Far Eastern Economic Review*, 14 November 1996.
161 Cf. *La dépêche internationale des drogues*, January 1998, p. 2. For other investment examples of the Chinese diaspora, cf. André et Louis Boucaud, *Le Monde diplomatique*, May 1996, p. 24.
162 Cf. *La Dépêche internationale des drogues*, November 1997, p. 2. OGD, Paris.
163 Cf. Radio Australia 3 November 1996, in SWB BBC Asia-Pacific, 5 November 1996, p. B.5.
164 Cf. *Far Eastern Economic Review*, 14 August 1997, p. 19.
165 Cf. *Nord-Sud Export Conseil*, Myanmar report, 20 September 1997, p. 34.
166 Cf. *Jane's Intelligence Review*, March 1998, quoted in Bertil Lintner, 'Global reach: drug money in the Asia Pacific', *Current History*, April 1998, p. 179.

167 Cf. *The China Business Review*, May–June 1994, p. 22.
168 Cf. *China Daily*, 15 July 1995, p. 10.
169 Cf. *China Daily*, 21 December 1994.
170 Cf. *Beijing review*, 2 September 1985, quoted in *Far Eastern Economic Review*, 22 December 1994.
171 Cf. Xinhua, 23 September 1994, in SWB BBC Asia-Pacific, 2 September 1994.
172 Cf. *The Times of India*, 10 March, 1996, p. 8.
173 Cf. *Far Eastern Economic Review*, 22 December 1994, p. 23 and 16 February 1995, p. 50; Li Peng press conference at Rangoun, SWB BBC Asia-Pacific, 31 December 1994.
174 Cf. *Far Eastern Economic Review*, 22 December 1994, p. 23.
175 Cf. *Xin Xiang ribao*, Bangkok, 10 January 1995, p. 8 in SWB BBC, 13 January 1995.
176 Cf. Bertil Lintner, *Far Eastern Economic Review*, 16 February 1995.
177 Cf. SWB BBC Asia Pacific, 29 December 1994.

3

The Socio-economic Stakes of Drug Trafficking

—◆—

The laundering matter

Far from being a perversion of capitalism, drug trafficking and money laundering may be interpreted as the continuation of the liberal rule of profit maximization at a time of globalization of trade. The Mafia order established at the level of drug production and distribution has all the attributes of an inverted state of law: it exerts a coercive power over a population or territory, with the sole objective of monopolizing the proceeds of one or more activities, and eliminating all competition. Its law is founded on threat and violence; its legitimacy is limited to the economic sphere of profit redistribution. Its power of attraction is proportionate to 'socio-cultural disintegration', as expressed by Pino Arlacchi:[1] a high unemployment rate, which targets the less favoured of the population, an absence of government attention, an increased gap between the consumer model, the valorization of economic success and the possibilities of acceding through legal means, all integrate to favour the development of a criminal labour force. These factors are reinforced in the Chinese case with the increase of socio-spatial and sectoral disparities, the deterioration of primary education in the villages since the 1980s,[2] and the disastrous examples which are regularly given by a very corrupted pluto-bureaucracy.

In contrast to the groups identified in the drug production and trafficking areas, laundering activities generate a strong interaction between the legal and illegal economy, consequently making it difficult to define borders. As explained by Philippe Leguet, 'apart from the drug trafficking, we also notice a character built in the activity of Mafia-type criminal organizations: their variety. In fact it consists of multiple-service criminal enterprises, from which it becomes extraordinarily difficult to distinguish the origins of licit revenues and those from illicit activities.'[3]

To the socio-cultural disintegration from the grassroots, one may add the corruption of certain representatives of the economic and political order, who are supposed, in fact, to personify the dominant values. The last decade of the twentieth century was characterized by a considerable extension of the 'grey zone' of the flow of suspect money, from fiscal evasions to occult commissions.[4] France, for example, as shown by Arnaud Mercier, provides

'multiple trafficking and dirty money influence in its relations with former African colonies. The successive French governments left African leaders to personally gain fortune with revenues from co-operation (let us note that a proportion of these funds returns to France in cash form so as to finance the election campaigns), or tolerate the advantages of their political entourage of doubtful African practices in order to enrich themselves and manage diverse import–export trafficking.'[5]

The development of this grey zone was contemporary with the accelerated growth of narco-dollars between 1985 and 1995, and the globalization process which reinforced the purely financial valorization of capital, independent from goods and services production.

If one considers the FATF (Financial Action Task Force) estimations, published after the G7 Summit in 1989, the

US$85 billion available each year for laundering is a small amount compared to the net international financing evaluated at US$6440 billion at the end of 1995; on the contrary, however, it is high in comparison to the US$400 billion accumulated since 1974 by the Gulf petroleum countries.[6] According to Pierre Kopp, the most reasonable estimation of the amount laundered each year is US$100 billion, an amount comparable to the black hole of the international balance of payments (US$120 billion) observed by the IMF.[7] This narco-profits evaluation is similar to the research conducted by the American Federal Reserve in 1984 and 1986, which estimates an amount of US$150 billion circulating to feed the American underground economy, the dollarization of certain countries, a section of international tourism, and illegal transactions in the world.[8] By the mid-1990s, there was an estimated US$185–260 billion cash dollars outside of the USA, in other words, 50–70 per cent of the total of green bills.[9]

Donald Regan, former American Secretary of the Treasury, publicly suggested the trade of bills so as to hinder trafficking, by trading the green for the blue. Interpreted as an extension of the public debt, this project was quickly abandoned: once deposited into the bank, most of the US$150 billion, which constitute non-paid debts for the American Treasury, would be converted into Treasury bonds paid at 8–10 per cent,[10] just as much of a loss to profit for Washington. The export of green bills clears the profitable margins record. According to Steve H. Hanke:

> the Federal Reserve prints and distributes small pieces of green paper without having interest to one single cost, and gains currency in exchange. This comes down to a loan without interest for foreign holders of green pieces of paper. The Fed then invests in products under the name of the federal government and reverses the profits to the American Treasury ... [considerable profits], between 11 and 15 billions of US dollars per year, in

other words an equal amount of federal receipts coming from inheritance rights and donations.[11]

At the end of the 1980s, most of these bills were intended for Latin America. Since then, Europe has become the dominant destination, with Russia absorbing more than half of foreign dispatches of US dollars, in other words almost US$20 billion in 1994. After Europe, the Far East and the Middle East today account for almost 30 per cent of the dispatches of US dollars.[12]

Along with these missing dollars, which helped to finance illegal flows, we may add yens, marks, pounds, and francs, 'which would surely be found missing, if any attention was paid to the matter', notes Stéphanie Brunys.[13] From this point of view, bad money indirectly contributes to a reduction in the public debt of large industrialized countries, one of the major problems of the Western States. Once introduced into the bank system, it may directly contribute to financing it as bond purchases.

The initial phase of drug money investment in bank establishments or non-traditional financial establishments (foreign exchange offices, stock brokers, art stores, jewellers, casinos, raw material brokers) constitutes the weakest link in the laundering chain.[14] The subsequent phase, which serves to lose track of illicit profit in a cascade of transactions, is facilitated by the flow of financial markets, raw material markets, by-product markets, options and trade markets – which together constitute daily transactions of US$1200 billion. The financial globalization achieved, thanks to the electronic transfers, allows the delocalization of high labour-intensive activities and the deterritorialization of trade. Thirty years ago, the economic interactions between countries were essentially in the form of the trade of products. Today, the international commerce of goods and services is increasingly dependent on the flow of direct and portfolio investments. The multiplication of screen companies and offshore havens,[15] often used by multinational groups for commission or fiscal evasion, or by larger financial centres such as London, New York or Tokyo,[16] favours the integration of narco-profits in the most speculative sectors of the legal economy, generally favoured by illicit capital: finance, real estate, tourism, gambling, works of art.

The financial globalization increases the channels of communication between legal and illegal activities, through the intermediary of painless banking. The deregulation of free trade makes the repressive arsenal against the drugs trade inefficient and problematic. In this hazardous environment, the narco-capitals navigate in a similar way to supertankers: they have constrained routes.[17] The measures adopted by the FATF had, until recently, the effect of increasing the profit margins perceived by the launderers, and encouraging the diversification of the traditional laundering activities centred in Europe, North America, Singapore and Hong Kong, all to the advantage of former communist countries.[18] David Andelman estimates that the cost of laundering services increased from 6 to 26 per cent of narco-profits, since this activity is considered a federal offence.[19] According to Patrick Glorieux, 'numerous superior bank executives, whether French or foreign, privately recognise that their respective establishments launder a great amount of unknown origin, by taking very high margins', in the region of 10 to 15 per cent, from which they must take the commission of the inter-mediaries, as much as 25 per cent for a 'heavy laundering'.[20] Less than 1 per cent of the 100 billion narco-dollars laundered annually is seized by specialized organizations, which are almost powerless in the face of criminal groups who are prepared to sacrifice up to 40 per cent of their profits to recycle their gains in the legal economy.[21] Under these conditions, the laundering of drug money 'practically remains unpunished', as underlined by Pierre Kopp.[22] In the name of the 'professional secret' and of 'non intervention', the intermediation of banks or non-bank establishments operates as a barrier between criminal groups and legal economies. The illicit capital is recycled with the same procedures as that derived from fiscal fraud. The financial system consists of a melting pot where the corrupt grey zone and the trafficking black zone flow together: 'corruption protects laundering, which nourishes in itself the corruption, in a financial spiral leading to an incessant and increasing criminalization of the economy.'[23]

In certain cases, such as the Italian Ambrosiano Bank or the Pakistani IBCC, the criminal groups have shown a preference for taking direct or indirect control of international financial organizations to facilitate their laundering operations. But these strategies can be identified, unlike the more common recourse to intermediaries or the purchasing of shares in international banks, which is the most recent and no doubt the most 'productive' trend.[24] According to the experts of the profession, French banks annually launder billions of dollars, and one may estimate the world narco-profit laundering benefits to be in the region of US$13–17 billion, distributed between banks and financial organizations.[25]

The statistics illustrate the limits of the repressive policy: in Europe and the USA, the annual profits from drug trafficking, evaluated at US$85 billion (according to the FATF), US$100 billion (according to the European parliament) and US$117 billion (according to the French Association of Banks), may generate, in one decade, interest that is seven times higher than the initial funds.[26] The revenues taken from these investments are considerable even when compared to those taken from trafficking. The Columbian traffickers repatriate, for example, between US$2 and 5 billion of cocaine profits in the American market, which represents between 4 and 9 per cent of the GDP of their country. Nevertheless, Francesco Thoumi was able to estimate that their capital stocks accumulated in Columbia and in foreign countries were between US$39 and 66 billion in 1990.[27] According to another similar evaluation, on an annual market of US$26 billion in the United States, the Columbian groups gathered at most US$6 billion. If they repatriate only US$2 billion, there would then remain 24 billion US dollars (92 per cent of narco-profits) available for laundering in the United States or elsewhere.[28]

This simple observation has serious implications for the analysis of the flow of money related to drug trafficking. The laundering banks and non-banking financial establishments can be seen as beneficiaries of the trafficking channel, in as much as they share the added value with a minimum of risk. In contrast to the production, trafficking and distribution of drugs, which mobilize a marginal workforce in a high risk environment, laundering activities mobilize strong and socially well-recognised operators, while they create no violence or obvious victims. As they use the same techniques, it is particularly difficult to distinguish the laundering of drug money from fiscal evasion, or from the irregular financing of political parties, or the recycling of funds from prostitution, gun trafficking or any other criminal activity. The banking profession has a tendency to take refuge behind this difficulty so as to discharge itself from all responsibility in cases of infractions of law and regulations with regard to narco-profit laundering.[29]

The role of offshore banking

The borders between the white zone of the legal economy, the grey zone of corruption and fiscal evasion and the black zone of the criminal economy diminish in a convergence of interests between Mafia groups, certain financial groups and certain politicians. The development of offshore banking, in parallel with financial deregulation, has considerably facilitated this process. We often associate it with fiscal paradises situated in the tropics, even when the reality is much more diverse. If we take a rigorous definition, the offshore financial centres receive funds in foreign currency from non-residents and lend them to other non-residents. Since this form of financial intermediation is provided solely to non-residents, through transactions that do not imply local currency, local authorities impose a minimum of taxes and financial regulation (for example, on the ratio of bank solvency).[30] The secrecy of transactions is generally guaranteed and there are legal refuges in case of pursuance. Since the reinforcement of financial and fiscal regulation in large industrialized countries, in the 1960s and 1970s, offshore centres have become more attractive for international operators. They have gradually begun to act as a crossroads for financial exchanges, to such an extent that more than half of the world's monetary transactions transit through them today.[31]

This situation is tolerated by the 'onshore' governments, as long as the offshore centres remain within their realm of influence and allow national enterprises to become more competitive on the international market. State supervisions may then control their own domestic operations.[32]

Offshore banking is generally used for three reasons: first it is used to place domestic international groups in a more advantageous fiscal environment where there is an absence of trade control. This is the case, for example, for maritime transport, or for the captive insurance industry, and it allows enterprises to cover their international risks at more advantageous local rates. Seventy-five per cent of the reinsurance world market is thus concentrated in offshore centres, through transnational corporations.[33] The second role of offshore banking consists of exploiting the opportunities of capital and currency markets in confidential and fiscal 'optimization' conditions, a euphemism signifying institutionalized fiscal evasion: in 1993, this is how banks managed US$1.5 trillion in offshore investments, representing 30 per cent of their assets in industrialized countries, and 22 per cent of their exterior world assets.[34] Apart from the banks, the considerable increase in offshore investment funds illustrates the development of these centres in the last two decades: in 1979, there were only 75 offshore investment funds; at the end of 1996, there were as many as 3314, in other words 44 times more.[35] As of 1993, offshore investment funds managed US$1 trillion in assets.[36] Finally, offshore centres are used to manage great fortunes, a third of which (US$5.5 trillion) are placed in offshore investments.[37]

According to operators such as MacKinsey and Co., a number of Swiss groups capture 35–45 per cent of the world offshore market, ahead of London (15 per cent), a group from the USA (15 per cent), Hong Kong and Singapore (10 per cent), Luxembourg (10 per cent) and the rest of the world (5–10 per cent).[38] These figures underline London's role as the principal offshore centre, the managing City, with its 450 foreign banks, and about US$1000 billion worth of funds which come from non-residents.[39] Not everyone agrees with this point. The IMF for example, does not consider Switzerland as the headquarters of offshore centres, but establishes its own ranking of the principal centres: the Bahamas (British), Bahrain, the Cayman Islands (British), Hong Kong, the Dutch West Indies, Panama and Singapore; then come the less important places such as Dublin, Cyprus (which counts 15 000 offshore companies according to the US State Department), Madeira, Malta, the Malaysian island of Labaun, and Bangkok.[40] To this highly restricted list, we must add, among others, the Bermuda Islands (British – specialising in insurance), Costa Rica and Panama, Uruguay, Liberia, Liechtenstein, Monaco, Andorra, Gibraltar, San Marino (Italy), Dubai, the Vanuatu Islands, Nauru, Western Samoa, Cook and Marshall Islands (Pacific), Mauritius, the Seychelles, Sirjan (Iran) and Shanghai, which has developed an offshore banking centre in the new district of Pudong.[41]

The Cayman Islands are often seen, quite credibly, as the prototype of fiscal havens serving as mail boxes for companies which do not have a physical presence: with a population of 33 000 and 550 banks represented (including 47 of the world's top 50) they manage more than US$500 billion worth of deposits, which make it the fifth financial centre of the world.[42] About 7 per cent of the world's transactions in eurodollars transit through the archipelago and 29 000 offshore companies are registered there.[43] Most of them are simple mail boxes that serve as a relay for international transactions. According to the American DEA, the invested funds in the Cayman Islands come mainly from the USA.[44] Local authorities presented the results of the anti-laundering legislation as of 1992: out of the 500 declarations of suspected transactions to this date, 80 per cent were identified as criminal.[45] However, the legislation of money laundering only concerns banks which have a physical presence, which constitute 10 per cent of registered establishments; the former inspector of the financial services transferred to the private sector by becoming the leader of the local operations of the Deutsch Morgan Grenfell Bank.[46] According to the American State Organization and the UNDCP, these regulation gaps, found to some extent everywhere in the region, explain the true industrial dimensions of the drug money laundering in the Caribbean, which can reach US$50 billion annually.

The flow of illicit money is increasingly facilitated by the transit function that offshore places play in the international financial system. In the shadow of the financial regulations, laws and tax systems of the large States that generate the flow initially, offshore banking enjoys an extra-territoriality, which is the reason for its existence. The size of legal markets related to financial deregulation in the 1980s and the progressive institutionalization of fiscal evasion have simultaneously become the essential weapons for laundering drug money: together they effectively dilute the not-insignificant amount of narco-dollars within a series of perfectly legal operations. A paradoxical situation has developed, as in the Channel Islands, where the search for respectability as an offshore centre makes a place 'even more attractive for the money launderers', according to the former head of financial regulations in Guernsey.[47]

The development of offshore activities reflects the more general gap between the globalization process of financial markets and their supervision, as ensured by the national bases. Nothing illustrates this contradiction better than the ways in which they unite London with dependent territories.

The island of Jersey, for example, manages the equivalent of US$370 billion, US$160 billion of which are placed in trust funds under administration, US$145 billion correspond to bank accounts and US$55 billion to collective investment funds. Most of this money comes from wealthy people, from companies and management funds, even though it is difficult to conclude their origin, according to the president of the Finance and Economy Committee. More than 60 per cent of these funds (US$243 billion) are invested in the capital markets of the City of London, which derive considerable advantages from these contributions.

Guernsey, the Isle of Man and Jersey deposits are not far from those of the Cayman Islands (US$480 billion), one-third of which comes from the UK, and more than half is probably reinvested in the London market.[48] The community of interest unanimously shapes a defensive line in the Jersey financial environment: it is generally agreed that money laundering can never be entirely controlled, and that London is without doubt its 'world capital'.[49] Simultaneously a member of the European Union and yet not submissive to its jurisdictions, the Channel Islands and the Isle of Man 'consist of good examples of a combination between a permissive regulation and an offshore status which makes an ideal place to hide illicit financial operations', according to a high ranking official of the Brussels Commission Anti-fraud unit.[50]

The situation in the Channel Islands is also seen in the last dependent territories of the British Empire, most of which are prosperous offshore centres, maintaining very close relations with the City of London (Turks and Caicos Islands, Cayman Islands, British Virgin Islands, Bermuda, Anguilla, Montserrat, Gibraltar). In order to avoid excessive criticism, London today tries to protect the British populations of these last remaining parts of the Empire, approximately 160 000 inhabitants, against financial regulation, by bringing them in line with the British criteria in the year 2000.[51]

Private banking is one of the most well-known markets and is closely linked to the offshore centres where great fortunes are managed. Estimates of the size and origin of this market vary: some underline that millionaires come equally from Europe, North America and Asia, especially Japan.[52] Its minimum amount is usually estimated at between US$8 and 10 trillion; US$2 or 3 trillion would find its way to offshore centres, a figure that simultaneously reveals the extreme concentration of wealth, and its propensity to escape from any type of regulation.[53] According to more precise evaluations the 'wealth market' could represent between US$15 and 17 trillion, US$5.5 trillion of which would be placed in offshore centres.[54] The profession manages more than 4000 organizations. The Swiss Banks Union, the Swiss Credit and the Swiss Bank Corporation, are the biggest intervening parties. They each manage approximately US$400 billion from private assets in this very lucrative market, almost half of which is concentrated in Swiss establishments: the profits were estimated at US$20 billion in 1996. This is a market which increases from two to three times more quickly than the concerned country's GDP, and therefore sharpens the competition and increases the number of intermediaries, such as First Boston, Citibank or the famous institutions of Wall Street.[55]

There are many indications that besides considerable fiscal evasion on a global level (the American Treasury estimates its leaks to be about US$70 billion per year), *offshore private banking* is often used to recycle drug money or money from other illicit activities. First, the annual amount of narco-dollars available for laundering (between US$85 and 117 billion) is far from being negligible with regard to the international financial system: it represents one-fifth of the world bonded market (the new issues of bonds were valued at US$512 billion in 1996) and one-third of the international bank credits (valued at more than US$300 billion in 1996).[56] Important financial needs, especially in high risk emergent markets, may converge with abundant investment offers, their discretion being more attractive than their actual productivity.

Second, the twofold increase in private offshore assets, from US$2300 billion to US$5500 billion (or US$5.5 trillion) between 1989 and 1996,[57] may only be explained by the strong economic development of certain zones or the high productivity of certain investments. The international expansion of drug trafficking is new and is centred in privileged geographic places, areas such as Latin America and Asia. A study made by Gemini Consulting and the American business bank Merrill Lynch, estimated that 6 million millionaires today controlled almost all the private banking assets with US$16 600 billion, or an average of US$2.7 million per depositor. During the last ten years, the Latin-American proportion of this private wealth has risen from US$1200 billion to US$2200 billion US dollars, feeding the rapid increase of offshore centres in the Caribbean, such as the Cayman Islands and the Bahamas.[58] We have already seen that the American State Organization and the UNDCP estimated a figure of US$50 billion for the annual laundering of drug money in this area. In Asia, the same study estimated the increase in private wealth to be 15 per cent per year during the last decade, representing US$3500 billion. As an offshore centre, Singapore would certainly benefit from this market and from the transfer of funds from Hong Kong (before the relinquishment of the British colony to China).[59] But the creation of a new centre, with the Bangkok International Offshore Banking Facility, in 1995, also attracted certain suspect funds to Thailand, a country known for its massive recycling of narco-dollars.

Third, the confidentiality assured to industry from private banking, combined with the legal protections supplied by offshore places, offers a maximum of guarantees against suspension, pursuit or the seizure of assets considered as illegal. The scandalous dissimulation, for over half a century, of the assets of Holocaust victims shows how even crimes against humanity can be accommodated within the 'sacrosanct' respect of 'bank confidentiality, an inalienable possession of Swiss banking', especially as it is defended by certain circles in Zurich.[60] The increase of private banking operators and competition in the business often incite operators to disregard the origin of their client's assets, including in the onshore areas where the regulations are supposed to control them. Interrogated on the numerous deposits of 20 to 70 million narco-dollars made by Raul Salinas, brother of the Mexican President, the regional official of the private banking sector of Citibank in New York declared to investigators that he would never have imagined investigating the provenance of these funds: 'it would be like asking a Rockefeller where their money came from'.[61]

Lastly, private bankers or fund managers sometimes find themselves being barely honest; for example, during a series of embezzlements that endangered the profession at Deutsch Morgan Grenfell of London, and the Hong Kong sector of the Jardine Bank and Flemings, more than 100 employees and managers directly or indirectly participated in the embezzlement of funds on profitable accounts of certain clients.[62]

The Financial Action Task Force of the G7 countries has, since 1989, considerably reinforced anti-laundering legislation. Most operators in the profession are aware of these new game rules, and the extent to which the banks may be accused in the absence of a guarantee on the origin of the funds invested in their company. According to American Congressmen, such as Spencher Bachus, one of the members of the banking committee of the House of Representatives, private banking is still perceived as a form of 'institutionalised laundering'.[63]

Offshore centres also play an important role in the development of 'Cyber-money' which has become, thanks to the Internet and smart cards, a more frequently used means of payment. Cash is always useful for illicit transactions, since it favours anonymity. To this traditional attribute, cyber-money adds the velocity of electronic individual transfers throughout the world by eliminating stock problems as well as the spill of bills and coins, a true headache for big traffickers.[64]

One Internet site, Global Financial Network, based in California, boasts that it 'treat[s] cash money that comes from *all* activities', and advertises 'its activities to dissimulate assets' in Antigua and the Isle of Man, and its capacity to 'help clients introduce their cash into the American Banking system, without anyone identifying its source, even … the government.' The European Union Bank, which presents itself as the first offshore bank on the Internet, offers 'fiscal protection programs in the Caribbean, tested by the international finance and trade community'. Antigua's American International Management Services takes a further step by selling not only banking services or society payments, but also 'permanent residence, passports and nationalities of Antigua, of Dominica and of St Kitts'.[65] Other 'entrepreneurs' from the Cook Islands, in the Pacific, created a *cyber-casino*, by organizing video versions of traditional games and deposits made by credit cards. Eighty per cent of the net profits return to the receiving company in Nevada.[66]

The advent of electronic commerce, estimated to represent US$70 billion in 2000, or 1 per cent of the world trade, according to the American authorities, also offers new possibilities for accounting manipulations and fiscal evasion, especially while international regulation in this domain is at an early stage. As two legal experts have illustrated,

> in an electronic environment, it is easier to delocalize one's activities, even to falsify one's identity so as to escape taxation. Thus a multinational firm may locate a server in a fiscal haven (in other words *cyber-haven*) to carry out its commercial activities without paying tax, throughout the entire world.[67]

In light of these fiscal evasion opportunities, cyber-payments associated with offshore centres may create favourable conditions for laundering of money. As long as they are not integrated in international accounting their increase may even weaken the monetary policy of Central Banks.[68]

A few years ago, one economist from the IMF had foreseen a relative decline in offshore banking, which he thought was caused by the decrease of their power of attraction in an international context of deregulation, and by the emergence of derivatives, increasingly concentrated in large financial centres.[69] On the contrary, it seems that there has been an acceleration of international investments, an increase in private banking and cyber-payments all favouring the off-shore places. Offshore banking, which allows the bypassing of national regulations at high speed, by creating a dual-speed global legal and fiscal system, has hence become an essential passage for international financial trade, and has greatly contributed to its criminalization.

Notes

1 Cf. Pino Arlacchi, *Mafia et compagnie: l'éthique mafiosa et l'esprit du capitalisme*, Presses Universitaires de Grenoble, 1986, pp. 240.

2 Between 1980 and 1994, the number of primary schools fell from 917316 to 682588, and the number of school children in primary education fell from 294 million to 253 million, while the Chinese population increased during the same period to 211 million (Cf. *China Statistical Yearbook*, 1995, pp. 585 and 590.)

3 Cf. Philippe Leguet, Office central de repression de la grande delinquance financière, 'Grande criminalité organisée: dessous et enjeux', *Relations internationales et stratégiques*, IRIS magazine, no. 20, Paris, Winter 1995.

4 Besides the Japanese example, where the financial scandals caused many Prime Ministers to resign, we may quote the investigations in France on the financing of the SDC, of the SP and of the Republican Party, as well as the 'hawalla scandal' in India, which caused the loss of the 1996 elections for the Rao government.

5 Cf. *Relations internationales et stratégiques*, no. 20, Winter 1995.

6 Cf. Bertrand Gallet, 'La grande criminalité organisée: facteur de déstabilisation mondiale?' *Relations internationales et stratégiques* no. 20, Winter 1995.

7 Cf. Pierre Kopp, *L'économie du blanchiment: détection, prévention et répression du blanchiment issu du trafic de drogues illégales*, Association of the financial economy, French funding body for public works and housing, Paris, 1995, p. 10.

8 'Changes in the use of transaction and cash from 1984 to 1986', *Federal Reserve Bulletin*, Washington, March 1987.

9 Cf. Steve H. Hanke, Johns Hopkins University, in *Rapport moral sur l'argent dans le monde*, Paris, 1996, p. 137.

10 Cf. Jean-François Couvrat, 'Argent sale', *La Tribune Desfossés*, 12 September 1994.

11 Hanke, *Rapport moral sur l'argent dans le monde*, p. 138.

12 Ibid., pp. 137–8.

13 Cf. Stéphanie Brunys, 'L'entreprise narco-trafiquante: structures et stratégies', BA thesis, University Paris 8, Saint Denis, 1995, p. 23.

14 Cf. *La lutte contre le blanchiment de capitaux*, Report of the Financial Action Group (GAFI) presided over by Denis Samuel-Lajeunesse, La Documentation française, 1990, pp. 91–8.

15 Cf. Jean Chesneaux, 'Les confettis de l'Europe dans le grand casino planétaire', *Le Monde diplomatique*, January 1996.

16 Cf. Kasauki Sono, 'Le cas du Japon', in Kopp, *L'économie du blanchiment*, 1995.

17 The image is by Jean Jacques Chiquelin, cf. *Libération*, 16–17 March 1985.

18 Kopp, *L'économie du blanchiment*, p. 11. In Europe, the principal centres for laundering are Zurich, Berne, Geneva, the French-Holland Islands of St Martin, the Malt Islands, Isle of Man, Jersey, Guernsey, Luxembourg, Liechtenstein, Monaco and Andorra.

19 Cf. David A. Andelman, 'The drug money maze', *Foreign Affairs*, July–August 1994, p. 98.

20 Kopp, *L'économie du blanchiment*, p. 60.

21 Cf. Patrick Glorieux, 'Le blanchiment en France', in Kopp, *L'économie du blanchiment*, p. 164.

22 Ibid., p. 17.

23 Cf. Patrick Glorieux, 'Le blanchiment de l'argent de la drogue' in Pierre Kopp, *L'économie du blanchiment*, p. 65. Cf. also Pino Arlacchi, *Corruption, Organized Crime and Money Laundering World Wide*, 1992.

24 Andelman, 'The drug money maze', p. 101.

25 Glorieux, 'Le blanchiment en France', p. 166.

26 Kopp, *L'économie du blanchiment*.

27 Cf. Rensselaer W. Lee, III, 'Global reach: the threat of international drug trafficking', *Current History*, May 1995.

28 Kopp, *L'économie du blanchiment*, p. 221. According to Francesco Thoumi, Columbian exports of cocaine are situated within a price range of US\$1.5 to 3 billion per year. (Cf. *Problèmes d'Amérique Latine*, no. 18, July–September 1995, p. 10.)

29 Glorieux, 'Le blanchiment en France', pp. 158 and 163.

30 Cf. M. Cassard, 'The role of offshore centres in international financial intermediation', IMF working papers, September 1994, p. 5.
31 Ibid., p. 4.
32 Ibid., pp. 2 and 22.
33 Ibid.
34 Cassard, 'The role of offshore centres'.
35 Cf. *Resident abroad*, 'The international investor in 1997', *The Financial Times Magazine*, p. 18.
36 Cassard, 'The role of offshore centres'.
37 Cf. below.
38 Cf. *Financial Times*, 22 January 1998, p. 8.
39 Cassard, 'The role of offshore centres', pp. 4 and 5. According to other more recent estimates, London generates US$600 billion of non-resident funds. Cf. *Financial Times*, 24–25 January 1998, p. 7.
40 Cassard, 'The role of offshore centres'.
41 Cf. *China Daily*, 16 February 1998.
42 Cf. George Graham, 'Grand Cayman fights off illicit image', *Financial Times*, 4 December 1996, p. 4.
43 Cassard, 'The role of offshore centres', p. 19.
44 Cf. DEA Report 1996.
45 Graham, 'Grand Cayman fights off illicit image'.
46 Cf. Ibid.
47 Graham, 'Grand Cayman fights off illicit image', p. 7.
48 Cf. *Financial Times*, 'Offshore financial review', 22 January 1998, p. 8.
49 Cf. *Financial Times*, 24–25 January 1998, p. 7.
50 Cf. *Financial Times*, 22 January 1998, p. 8.
51 Cf. *Financial Times*, 5 February 1998, p. 12.
52 Cf. *Far Eastern Economic Review*, Focus: Investing offshore/ Private banking, 15 May 1997, p. 44; 'Private banking: Japan', *Financial Times*, 26 November 1997. According to these statistics, Japan has 600 000 great fortunes, half of which are from trade, two-thirds of those in the USA, and the equivalent of those in France and Germany together.
53 For these estimations, cf. Tom Walker, 'Managing millionaires', *Sunday Morning Post*, Hong Kong, 28 April 1996, p. 6.
54 Cf. George Graham, 'Private banking, wealth market', *Financial Times*, 26 November 1997, p. 2.
55 Cf. William Glasgall and Alison Rea, *Business Week*, taken from *Le Courrier international*, 4–10 July 1996, pp. 28–9; Michael Prest, 'Private banking', *Financial Times Survey*, 26 November 1997.
56 Cf. 'Les marchés internationaux de capitaux en 1996', Banque des Règlements Internationaux (IRB), in *Problèmes économiques*,

24 September 1997. The net international financing was estimated by the IRB at US$6640 billion at the end of 1995: *Problèmes économiques*, 18 September 1996.

57 Prest, 'Private banking', p. 5.

58 Cf. George Graham, 'Wealth market', *Financial Times*, 26 November 1997, p. 2.

59 Ibid.

60 Cf. *Le Monde*, 30 July 1997, p. 2.

61 Cf. *Le Monde*, 16 January 1998. 30 September 1996, p. 20.

62 Cf. *Le Monde*, 10 September 1996, p. 17; *Financial Times*, 30 September 1996, p. 20.

63 Cf. *Financial Times*, 26 November 1997.

64 Cf. DEA Report 1996.

65 Cf. *US News and World Report*, 28 October 1996.

66 Cf. Radio Australia external service, Melbourne, 16 June 1997, in SWB BBC Asia-Pacific, 18 June 1997.

67 Cf. Marie Antoinette Coudert and Daniel Arthur Laprès, 'Quelle fiscalité pour le commerce électronique?', *Droit fiscal* 1997, no. 46–7, p. 1353.

68 Cf. 'Can cybermoney affect monetary policy?', *Viewpoint*, Commerzbank's focus on German and European economic issues, December 1997.

69 Cassard, 'The role of offshore centres'.

4

Japan: The *Yakuza* Recession

—◆◆◆—

The case of Japan provides a very clear illustration of progressive financial criminalization and its consequences. Japan is a country which, simultaneously, is the second world economic power, the first creditor of the planet and the great organizer of the east Asian regionalization, through its direct investments, its transfers of technology and by commercial flows.

Known as the greatest economic and non-Western success, Japan is a developmental model for its neighbours, progressively diffusing its industrial know-how towards the new industrialized countries (Hong Kong, Singapore, Taiwan, South Korea), then towards the southeast Asian countries and China. The internationalization of the Japanese economy, representing in itself 70 per cent of east Asia's gross domestic product, seems to have reached maturity: in 1996, the level of Japanese products manufactured abroad (US$390 billion) surpassed its exports (US$380 billion).[1]

This economic power contrasts with the fragility of its financial system in the 1980s. The abundance of cash issued from export revenues, allied with excessive anticipation, has favoured a speculative environment: a terrifying increase of stock rates, the price of real estate and the art market. At the peak of the euphoria, on 31 December 1989, the Japanese stock market represented 42 per cent of the world stock capitalization, against 15 per cent in 1980, and 151 per cent of the GDP, against 29 per cent in 1980.[2] As for land and property prices, they sometimes surpassed US$160 000 per square metre, making it impossible for investment profits, whatever the use of land.[3]

Japan had eight of the ten leading world banks, and controlled one-quarter of the California Bank industry, 10 per cent of bank assets in the USA and as much as 25 per cent in Great Britain.[4] But the inflation of assets was followed by a less spectacular deflation, which caused the most severe Japanese economic recession since the Second World War, despite six successive economic revival plans.[5] Japan had to wait until the mid-1990s, and the Kobe earthquake, to finally lift the curtain of economic underworld implications, of strange relationships between business and crime.

During the second half of the 1980s, the alliance between politicians, technocrats and chiefs of enterprises, the famous 'iron triangle' which had forged the bases of the Japanese development, was transformed thanks to Mafia investments in the speculative sectors of the legal economy. Organized crime has a very well-defined social status in Japan. The authorities have, for a long time, valued the deviation structure as the reason for an exceptionally low delinquency rate. From police sources, it is possible to count 88 600 *yakuzas* belonging to 3300 different groups, most of which are affiliated to one of the three principal gangs: the Yamaguchi-Gumi, which numbers about 30 000 members mainly based in the region of Kansai (Osaka–Kobe–Kyoto), the Inagawa-kai, with 8000 members, and Suniyoshi-kai, having 6000 members.

The *yakuzas* participate in legal activities allowing them to recycle their traditional operating profits: first gambling, with the vogue of electronic billiards, the 'pachinkos', which in 1996 generated receipts of 25 000 billion yen, or almost 1.5 times the turnover of the Japanese automobile industry and 6.7 per cent of the GDP. Their illicit activities include prostitution, with a network covering the whole of Eastern

Asia and certain countries of Latin America such as Columbia, the extortion of funds, gun trafficking and drug trafficking. The consumption of metamphetamines illegally produced in South Korea or in China involved 500 000 people, and the consumption of cocaine about 150 000 people, in a population of 125 million.[6] Products such as heroin are less often consumed, due to a tacit agreement between the *yakuza* and the police, who prohibited the distribution of these substances on national territory, and imposed serious sentences. Police sources reveal that the illegal receipts of the *yakuza* could reach at least US$10 billion, maybe even more, one-quarter or one-third of which would come from drug trafficking.[7] These amounts, important in absolute terms, remain relatively negligible within a legal economy which had a gross domestic product of US$4 600 billion in 1997. But the gradual uptake of Mafia assets into the economy was to modify the picture.

Real estate, and especially land ownership, which may represent 80 or 90 per cent of operational prices[8] in very mountainous and dense regions (where only a quarter of the ground surface is habitable), constitutes a traditional financial asset for political parties. The regional public agencies utilize a system of invitation to tender for all operations, setting aside offers below their own estimate, and favouring the discrete distribution of contracts to 'registered' operators. The re-billing is transferred in terms of commissions that feed the black market of the parties. This represents a surcharge of 8–12 per cent covered by the taxpayer.[9] Certain politicians may be financed directly by real estate companies, through the manipulation of stock rates, as was seen during the Recruit-Cosmos scandal, when the Takeshita government fell in 1989.[10]

In January 1995, an earthquake in Kobe, which resulted in 5000 victims and more than US$100 billion worth of damage, revealed the irresponsibility permitted by this system which had allowed a loosening of construction control and a lack of respect for anti-earthquake precautions. The Japanese have become accustomed to this form of corruption, induced by the absence of any change in the holders of political power. 'During the long reign of the Liberal Democratic party [1955–93]', underlines Jean-Marie Bouissou, '9 out of 15 Prime Ministers were implicated or charged for scandals at one time or another during their career.'[11] But the subsequent trauma in Kobe revealed the speculative euphoria of the 1980s, and implication of the criminal underworld in the speculative activity of the legal economy: real estate, the stock market and works of art.

The example of Susumu Ishii, head of Inagawa-kai, the second largest Japanese criminal organization, is quite eloquent. This group lends US$2.5 billion to Sagawa Kyubin's group, which is partly invested in stockbroker firms such as Nomura and Nikko, and partly in investments in New York and in Texas, by hiring ex-President Bush's own brother, Prescott Bush, as a consultant![12] The rest of Sagawa Kyubin's funds contribute to financing the Liberal Democratic Party through the intermediary of the ex-godfather of Japanese politics, the vice-president of the LDP, Shin Kanemaru.[13]

But it is mostly in the real estate business that there is convergence between the banks and organized crime. As the analyst Koyo Ozeki has observed, 'the speculative bubble destroyed the walls set up between the formal and informal economies'.[14] Attracted by the opportunities for profit from a rising real estate market, the banks created subsidiary companies for housing, called the *jusen*, which give high risk loans to Mafia promoters, who expel people who get in the way of their operations either by intimidation or violence. Rebellious executives of the *jusen* are satisfied, if necessary, by prostitutes provided by their parent company.[15] The trade prospered until the Bank of Japan raised its interest rates to calm speculative fever, thereby launching the fall of the real estate market which precipitated the economic recession in 1991. The credit societies, who bought at high market prices in the 1980s, are incapable of reimbursing half of their loans, which are estimated at US$130 billion.

In 1995, the bad loans of the *jusen* became heavier with the continual fall in real estate prices. They rose from US$65 billion to US$97 billion (¥9700 billion), about 70 per cent of which is attributed to the *yakuza*.[16] The situation is further complicated by the involvement of agricultural co-operatives, members of the strong lobby animated by the Liberal Democratic Party, who financed landowner operations of the *jusen* up to US$52 billion.[17] The Ministry of Finance, one of the pillars of Japanese technocracy, is also involved in the scandal. High-level civil servants in the Ministry remained ignorant of the doubtful activities of the *jusen*, and did not hesitate, as Christian Sautter wrote, 'to resign from civil service jobs and work for eminent people in the private sector', even supporting, jointly with the Minister of Agriculture, the pursuit of their own operations after the strict credit control measures of 1990–91.[18]

The burst of the speculative bubble and the free fall of real estate prices, which may go as low as one-third of the value of the 1980s, precipitated the payments of significant accounts. Japanese banks showed bad debts, estimated at the end of 1995 at US$500 billion (¥50 trillion), 60 per cent of which (US$300 billions) are unlikely to be reimbursed, or the equivalent of a dozen Crédit Lyonnais if we use the latest estimations.[19] But these evaluations are often disputed: according to the Swiss Banks Union, the total of bad debts increased to US$688 billion.[20] The adoption of American accounting norms by the Japanese Banks Federation temporarily suspended the debate. The bad debts were estimated at the end of 1997 at ¥76 710 billion, in other words US$753 billion, representing 16 per cent of Japanese GDP and 12 per cent of bank credits. Of all of these debts, ¥11 400 billion (US$90 billion), in other words 15 per cent of the total, is considered as partially or totally reimbursable according to official statistics.[21]

The former director of criminal affairs at the National Police Agency, Raisuke Miyawaki, estimates that 10 per cent of the bad debts are related to the *yakuza* and that a supplementary 30 per cent have doubtful associations with organized crime.[22] In the weakest hypothesis, the non-recoverable gangster debts were set at about US$75 billion, an amount which corresponds to the *jusen* debts with Mafia associations (US$68 billion).[23] At the highest estimate, where 40 per cent of bad loans are directly or indirectly attributed to organized crime, the figure represents more than US$300 billion, or 6.5 per cent of the GDP of 1996. This estimate corresponds to the official statistics for non-recoverable debts. It gives an idea of the impact of the criminalization of the economy in a large industrialized country, and the systemic stakes which surround the liquidation of liabilities created by speculative tendencies.

During the 1995–1996 fiscal year, Japanese banks were constrained to put aside US$97.5 billion to deposit funds into the bad debt account,[24] equivalent to the funds subtracted from investment. The interest rates on deposits did not stop decreasing, effecting an important transfer of bank savers' resources and facilitating the improvement of their debts. The taxpayers were also solicited to pay the bills of the 'unknown' speculators, since US$7 billion (¥685 billion) was allocated in the 1996 budget to absorb a part of the insolvent debts of the *jusen*, to the detriment of taxpayers.

These reorganisational measures, along with six programmes for new public spending (1992–1995, four of which had budgets superior to two per cent of the GDP),[25] limited the impact of the recession but without managing to restore confidence. The bankruptcy of regional banks and credit organizations increases with the decrease in land prices, which were used as collateral for about 70 per cent of credits in the speculative euphoria years.[26] As of 1997, the hastened investigations by the Commission of Stock surveillance operations revealed once again new relations between the financial sector, industrial sector and organized crime. The four famous enterprises, Nomura, Daiwa, Nikko and Yamaichi, which dominate the Stock Market in Tokyo, the second largest bank of Japan, the Dai-Ichi Kangyo Bank, the Mitsubishi group and 20 other large companies (including Hitachi and Dai Nippon Printing) were implicated in the '*sokaiya*' scandal.[27]

The financial and industrial groups used gangster services to assure themselves of general shareholder consensus assemblies (in Japanese called '*sokai*'), by intimidating, with implicit threats of violence, the troublemakers or the amateurs with troublesome questions. But one part of the '*sokaiya*' had turned the system to their advantage, by threatening the enterprises into revealing sensitive information. This fund embezzlement system was extraordinarily lucrative for the thousands of *yakuzas* involved. As an example we may consider Ryuichi Koïke, the most famous among the *yakuza*, whose trial in Tokyo in December 1997 revealed the system.

Born in 1943 in Niigita, a city at the centre of the archipelago, Koïke began his career as a small street seller before joining a *yakuza* organization in Tokyo. As of 1968, he was known to be making a move against the leftist movements, with the Mitsubishi Heavy service, a supplier for the Japanese army. Rikiya Kijima, one of the godfathers of the underworld, took Koïke under his protection and introduced him to the world of trade, where he quickly became known and feared by the great leaders who resorted to his services. During his trial, Koïke admitted to having extorted more than US$100 million from the four largest brokerage companies and from the DKB.[28]

During 1997, there were arrests of presidents such as Hideao Sakamaki of the Nomura firm, Fujita of the Daï-Ichi Kangyo Bank, a suicide by the former president of the same establishment plus the resignation of leaders of the four largest Japanese brokerage companies – all caught up in the '*sokaiya*' scandal. The scandal demonstrated the ascendancy of the invisible relations which paralysed the stabilization of bad debts by the bank and credit companies. This occurred despite all the sacrifices made by the population in terms of investment falls and decreases in growth, falls in savings payments and new fiscal contributions related to the rise of public expenses and budgetary deficits, representing 7 per cent of the GDP. The practices of the *sokaiya* illustrate to what extent 'the number one rule in Japan is not to mention the invisible rules'.[29]

It became clear that the banks, the large companies and certain industrial groups had become true hostages of the *yakuzas*, which refused to reimburse their bad real estate debts and even received new loans: this was the case for Ryuichi Koïke, who signed up US$100 million worth of credit with the DKB bank between 1994 and 1996, even though all the evidence strongly suggested that these funds would never be reimbursed.[30] This was also the situation with the great Yamaichi society, which gave Koïke US$654 000 of profits brought out from the currency market of Singapore.[31] Similarly for Mitsubishi Motors, accused of having deposited US$191 000 with the '*sokaiya*' Terubo Tei.[32]

These 'credits' or deposits for 'service loans' hide a vast system of debt cancellation and fund embezzlement accompanied by physical threats and blackmail over sensitive revelations. First of all, the *yakuzas*, having speculated on the increase in real estate, speculated in turn on its decrease. In Tokyo, the price of commercial land decreased by 70 per cent and the residential land prices by 45 per cent from their peak in 1990.[33] In the archipelago, the payment of bad real estate debts, 70 per cent of which were related to *yakuzas*' interests, was virtually blocked. Between 1993 and 1995, 20 violent attacks against financial executives were recorded, including the execution of two bankers from the Sumitomo and Hanwa Bank, who were responsible for collecting debts.[34] The new strategy of downward speculation inaugurated by gangsters was to oppose (by visible occupations) the sale of real estate goods which served as collateral for 70 per cent of the bank loans. The *yakuza* thus acted as service providers on behalf of companies under liquidation, and in their own interest, the idea being that they could thereby acquire, at the lowest price, buildings depreciated by their very presence.[35] According to police officials, this situation has been used particularly in Kansai (the Osaka–Kyoto–Kobe region), the Yamachi-Gumi kingdom, where about half of the enterprises maintain relations with the underworld.[36]

The progressive investments of the *yakuzas* in real estate and well-known companies thus drove them in a vicious circle, paralysing the improvement of the financial sector and the tentative hope of economic revival. It is for this reason that this – the longest economic stagnation that Japan has ever seen since the Second World War – is known as the '*yakuza* recession', so nominated by the former director of Criminal Affairs of the National Police Agency.[37] This remark does not remove the responsibility of the business environment in the speculative euphoria period as during the depreciation of assets.

Certain bankers are in no hurry to pay off the landowner or real estate assets, and may put up with the strategy, retaining *yakuzas'* goods while they wait for better days.[38] One of them declares without cynicism that

> 'the State took billions of taxes on the added-value of lands. It is normal that the public money serves to eliminate the liabilities of the *jusen*. In any case, the debts are irretrievable: to cover 10 per cent we would have to spend half of the money with the judicial procedure. This is not worth it.'[39]

For his part, the godfather of Kyoto, Takayama, insists on the responsibilities of the business sector: 'often, we have just worked at the demand of banks or promoters who are still hungrier than us. We are not the ones that gained the most. Many enterprises are more offending than us.'[40]

This point of view is not necessarily over-simplistic. The embezzlement of *sokaiya* funds, for example, is inseparable from the well-known practice of the *tobashi* or 'non-appraisal', which allows the dissimulation of the loss of enterprises to stockbrokers and clients by dividing offshore accounts. In November 1997, the most resounding failure of the postwar period, that of the fourth-largest Japanese business, the Yamaïchi Company, with accumulated losses of ¥260 billion (US$2.1 billion), was turned around with an intervention which did not appear on its consolidated balance sheet. The deficits were bought by a subsidiary company based in the Cayman islands...

This unsurprising information was accumulated by three supervision organizations, the Ministry or Finance, the Bank of Japan and the Stock surveillance Commission, while rumours of the deception of the group, which ran about for six years, provoked this caustic comment by a financial consultant in Tokyo: 'it is a little like the guy in the movie *Casablanca* saying that he is surprised at finding gambling inside of a casino.'[41]

The *sokaiya* gangsters embezzled funds from different groups with the help of sensitive information concerning the falsification of balances; this illustrates the permissiveness of supervision bodies. It quickly appears, in fact, that the dissimulation of the Yamaïchi losses, the assets of which were estimated at US$27.9 billion, took advantage of the complicity indulged in by the civil servants of the Ministry of Finance in charge of controlling banks and large well-known companies. The suicide of two officials, who had accepted multiple invitations, golf games or sexual services from supervised financial organizations, reveals the quite wide-spread connections of the public relations departments of financial organizations within the Ministry of Finance. If this system was quickly called into question after the scandal, with the inspection of 500 financial civil servants and 600 members of the Bank of Japan,[42] it was then transformed with another which reinforced the collusion between the controllers and the controlled: re-employment in the private sector of numerous financial civil servants after their retirement. In 1997, 24 of them had found jobs with banks, and 100 of them were working in different financial establishments.[43]

The question of the regulation of the financial system came back to the centre of the political debate, with the nomination of a new Finance Minister who decided to take the inspection responsibilities away from its ministry, and give them to a new agency. In the meantime, the confidence of savers and investors was undermined by the scandals. On top of the deflation of landowner assets, which had weighed down the bad bank debts, was added a 30 per cent fall in the Stock Market rate in the second half of 1997. The Asian crisis also weakened the credits of Japanese establishments in west Asia, valued at US$298.7 billion by the Bank of International Settlements. Half of these engagements, which represented less than 10 per cent of the total of the Japanese bank balances, were carried out in Hong Kong, in Indonesia, in South Korea and in Thailand. But at the end of the year, when the Nikkei index remained below 16 000, the higher latent values of the financial establishments only represented a few billion US dollars. The deposit of funds for these new bad debts may therefore consume almost the totality of the net bank assets which exceed the 8 per cent prudential ratio. Their operational margin is practically nil.[44]

The mistrust of private Japanese savers, whose total deposits are estimated at US$9700 billion, the second highest in the world, has led to a removal of bank deposits and financial assets to the benefit of postal savings, which also represent one-third of the domestic market, or to famous American firms that are well established on the Tokyo Stock Market.[45] To deal with the destabilization of the financial system, the government had reserved ¥13 trillion of public funds (US$102 billion) through the intermediary of the Bank of Japan, to re-capitalize the insolvent banks.[46] This exceptional rescue plan, which represents more than ten times the registered amounts of the 1996 budget to cover one part of the liabilities of the real estate co-operatives (*jusen*), shows clearly that Japan is embarking on perhaps the first-ever taxpayer-financed debt 'forgiveness' of a nation's criminal underworld, according to *Business Week*.[47]

The public funds released at this time, compared to the US$100 billion advanced to South Korea to pay its debts, can be absorbed by a system that has private savings of US$9700 billion. But the size of this mobilization, which corresponds to approximately 4 per cent of the State budget, explains Japan's low profile prior to the Asian crisis of 1997, very different from the engagements undertaken by the United States with regard to Mexico, in 1994–95. It also underlines the direct cost of economic investments by criminal groups which transform themselves into political issues.

The economic institutionalization of the *yakuzas* in the 1980s may in fact be explained by the financial need of a political system which is without doubt the most expensive in the world. The average cost of an election has quadrupled in Japan in 15 years. It was established at least ¥300–400 million (US$3–4 million at 1995 prices) at the end of the 1980s, whereas the maintenance of an electoral fief in the cultural framework of the 'gift civilisation' boils down another US$1 million per year. Japanese political personnel are estimated to spend more than ¥900 billion (US$9 billion) annually while the legally declared amount from donors does not exceed ¥356.9 billion (US$3.5 billion). 'We may then conclude', according to Jean-Marie Bouissou, 'that two thirds of the money that enters the political system is black money: *urakane* (money through the back door)'.[48] The construction sector, where the *yakuza* are still well entrenched thanks to the framework of its daily labour force,[49] the real estate sector and the stock market consist of privileged points of convergence between the political groups and the gangsters. The Sagawa Kyubin scandal (1992), which led to the temporary fall of the Liberal Democratic Party, illustrated this convergence, personified by the famous Shin Kanemaru, the true godfather of Japanese politics, who was swiftly put into hiding during the political part of the investigation.[50] Other more recent examples show to what extent relationships are maintained between the centre of power and the stock exchange.

Shokei Arai, official of the Liberal Democratic Party committee and in charge of the stabilization plan for the financial system based on public funds, resigned and then committed suicide following the serious accusations made against him: this former civil servant of the Ministry of Finance had opened an account under a false name, with his broker Nikko, which would have paid him about US$325 000, thanks to illegal transactions. 'Why me, when many hundreds are doing the same thing?' he declared in front of the Parliamentary Investigations Commission, the day before his suicide.[51] The fate of Shokei Arai seemed to affect many of his colleagues. Over and above the financial cost, taken from taxpayers and affecting the entire population, the succession of scandals and embezzlements finally put the legitimacy of the political system into question, in front of a public disoriented by the ascendency of corruption and organized crime.

Lessons from the Japanese crisis

What strikes us in the process we have just described is the length of its maturation, the slow emergence of scandals that hid the weakness of governments and the decreasing effect of the justice system. If all of the observers were aware of the corruption that existed, none of them, apart from the police and judiciary, noticed its new dimension which indeed took the form of a criminalization of the economy. Observers sometimes evoke the 'Mafia', but its action is always considered as marginal, incapable of affecting the regulation of the system. The Japanese recession, qualified as being 'complex' by economists such as Yoshikazu Miyazaki,[52] is essentially attributed to the burst of the speculative bubble and the increase in value of the yen against the dollar, shrinking the export market at the beginning of the 1990s. But this argument does not hold when we consider the decrease of the yen which lost more than 25 per cent of its value between 1995 and the end of 1996, increasing Japanese commercial surpluses. When the relations between the official economy and the underworld are recognized, conventional wisdom maintains that the public pressure and the liberalization programmed into the financial system will stabilize the situation by introducing transparency and competition.[53] In short, the stagnation is often considered from its purely economic dimensions, without taking into account the politics of successive governments and the strategies of the actors who refused to acknowledge the problems, but instead rested their hopes on a hypothetical return of growth to clear the bad debts.[54]

Each of these reports is true, to an extent, but they do not take into account the role of the criminal underworld when it comes to the freezing of the banks' liabilities. If the weight of organized crime remains marginal to the official economy, it is indubitable that its strategy may deeply affect the regulation of the system by retarding, in this case, the necessary adjustments for the return to healthy growth.

The mechanism of the formal economy has not taken hold, since a number of actors and criminal elements have managed to get a toe-hold, *by modifying the rules of the game.* Their clearly predatory logic serves to divert any financial intermediation to its own advantage, by undermining the confidence upon which it is founded. With the accumulation of irrecoverable debts, the violent predator appears to be in more than just indirect mode. The debts are taken back to the banks and credit establishments, which socialize the 'losses', corresponding in fact to gangster debts. One thus reaches a paradoxical situation where the stabilization of bad debts, borne by the taxpayers, indirectly pays for the criminal capital and constitutes a subsidy for embezzlement. The collectivization of the losses is followed by a privatization of Mafia benefits, within the framework of the *yakuza* strategy for the retention or the investment of depreciated assets.

What is problematic at this point, is the ingredients with which, from their accumulation and their new order, this new qualitative situation has been created. The first among them relies on the existence of a professional political system, increasingly costly, and simply financed by the illegal commissions on the public markets. One finds here a structural corruption tolerated in certain measure by the public. It also exists elsewhere: the General Secretary of the European Union estimated a surcharge of between 10 and 15 per cent related to corruption in the supply of goods and services in Europe.[55] The second element applies to the implicit legitimization of organized crime, based on an historic heritage (the *yakuza* tradition and the utilization of gangsters against the communist movements during the Cold War), and supported either by security arguments (the role of the Mafia in the framework of delinquency) or by populist ones (the social promotion opportunities that it offers in among disenfranchised populations).

The third ingredient, depending on the economic conjuncture, concerns the high risk business opportunities in certain sectors of development such as finance or real estate, where the capital appreciation may be particularly rapid. The fourth element, which Japan shares with France, is the straight overlapping between the high finance administration, the private financial sector and the political system. The institutionalized associations between the public and the private, the interested permissiveness of certain financial organizations' supervisors, created an environment that was favourable to drifts in a deregulation context.

Organized crime simultaneously exploits opportunities which are presented by each point of the triangle and the complicity which unites them. The management of legal and illegal activities (such as drug trafficking) frees masses of dirty money, which may in part be recycled into the political system, in order to buy indispensable protection from the underworld. In the real estate or stock domain, the *yakuza* passes from the status of subcontractor or service provider to the status of principal and blackmailer, where, once established in the workings of the system, it threatens to reveal the secrets of the opaque arrangements, which concealed the extent of the deflation of assets from savers. Their targeted interests seem to coincide with those of the political world, who find that the only immediate solution to the crisis is indeed the collectivization of losses from bankrupt organizations, without even questioning the privatization of Mafia benefits. At the same time, this rescue erodes the confidence of savers who mistrust the financial intermediation, and the confidence of the taxpayers, who are called upon to finance the deficits. The intervention of an independent judiciary and efficient financial supervision would be able to re-establish the confidence of the public previously enslaved to a predatory economic logic. The financial destabilization related to the criminal process, even if it remains limited and manageable with regard to the power of the system, definitely poses a legal, institutional and political problem.

Some observers minimize this non-economic view of the question by insisting on the 'oligopolistic and collusive' character of Japanese capitalism, 'which only *seems* to have opened to free market economics'.[56] The liberalization of the financial market, programmed for 2001 as part of the 'big bang', was to undermine the foundations of network capitalism in favour of market capitalism, and opacity was to give way to transparency. Nevertheless, this argument is impaired by a number of factors.

First, the bankruptcy of banks and the rescue plans founded on a socialization of losses are not only a Japanese speciality. The same situation was able to come about in much more competitive environments such as the USA (1981–92), in France (1992–95), in Norway (1987–93), in Finland (1987–93), in Sweden (1987–93) and in the UK (1987–94), by generating totals for aid or bad debts estimated at 8.8 per cent of the GDP at the end of the period for the USA, 1.3–3.6 per cent of GDP in the French case, and respectively for the others, 3.3 per cent, 15 per cent, 6 per cent and 2.3 per cent of GDP.[57] Faced with the macro-economic size of these failures, specialists of the financial system denounce the difference between the norms of supervision, prisoners of the national executive, and the need for a system which no longer identifies its borders.[58] Financial liberalization has considerably increased the risk for establishments in the absence of international supervision criteria. New tendencies intervene to make the world of finance the Achilles' heel of the globalized economy.

We must first invoke the weight of the large private actors, such as J.P. Morgan, in the elaboration of the prudential norms fixed by the Bank of International Settlements, which leads one to 'question oneself on the pertinence of the control procedures greatly influenced by them'.[59] The second new element applies to the emergence, in an international environment characterized by deregulation and the increase of competition, of financial conglomerates which regroup the bank activities, the insurances and brokering houses. These 'bank–insurance' organizations represent a true 'prudential challenge', to the extent that the borders between the different activities are mixed, whereas the risk control for each one is not at the same level. The differentiated levels of supervision within the same group 'allow us to anticipate the possibility of active strategies of bypassing regulation via appropriated group structures, in other words that are sufficiently opaque'.[60] Here, we immediately think of the possibilities offered by offshore centres and the 'off-balance' accounting which can cause the damage we have seen in the Japanese case.

The third new element is the high profile of derivative products on the international financial market. Derivatives (futures, options, swaps) first arose from contacts between operators hostile to risks and speculators willing to take them on. After beginning on American commodity exchanges, where they served to counter excessive variations in the value of raw materials by referring to future sales prices, derivatives found new applications in the 1970s, when financial instability arose from fluctuating currencies. Their scope was enlarged to protect the operators against interest rate and exchange risks. The financial deregulation wave of the mid-1980s extended application of futures to prevent risks on the financial markets, by not only betting on the future of currency stocks and the rent of money, but also on the indexes of large stock places, on the value of bonds given by medium- and long-term governments. The notional amount of actual contracts passed from approximately US$3000 billion in 1986 to US$50 000 billion in 1995.[61]

The paradox of these innovations, the sophistication of which reserves a quasi-monopoly in large financial centres, is that the anxiety to reduce risks seems to increase them, from the accumulation of virtual transactions. The fall of Barings Bank in 1995, due to the careless manipulations of a young trader in Singapore, who insisted on betting on an index recovery of Tokyo stock, in the period of the bursting of the financial bubble, illustrated the permissiveness or the failure of the internal management system risks of large establishments.

But beyond this particular case, the IMF has underlined the systemic financial risks related to the largest and most complex market for derivatives, the over-the-counter market. The active participation in this unlisted market may make the situation of an establishment more opaque for various reasons: the positions of these products are in the off-balance areas, which immediately limits the transparency of the information; most of the accounting norms are still not adapted to the flow of revenues and to the risks of these new products; it is difficult to evaluate the risks of the positions on the derivatives in the absence of information on the brokerage strategy of a company; the value of these products may vary in line with that of the underlying bonds, thereby affecting the portfolio value of an establishment; finally the unlisted derivatives are negotiated in a private context to answer to needs of a specific contract, allowing numerous counterparts to intervene in different countries.[62]

The opacity and the sophistication of derivatives markets, reserved for experts, not only create a potential destabilization factor in the financial system, but also create a criminalization factor of capital trade. Romeo Ciminello showed, from a series of concrete examples, how the international market in derivatives, and especially its 'over the counter' branch, offers ideal conditions for the laundering of a considerable amount of funds issuing from drug trafficking: the assets may be displaced without any worry, all by creating 'made-to-measure' operations adapted to particular cases. In his work *Un monde sans loi*, Jean de Maillard illustrated a number of derivatives laundering cases.[63] Police investigations and arrests confirmed that the new financial instruments, mainly the *financial futures*, were used to recycle a large quantity of narco-dollars.[64]

These diverse remarks on the international financial system thus serve to invalidate the neo-liberal argument, according to which liberalization may solve corruption problems. The reign of competition, which thrives with the globalization of markets, is far from being related to transparency, which resorts to an extra-economic, institutional and legal logic. On the contrary, today we notice a reinforcement of opacity: first caused by the influence of offshore centres, which reinforce the secrecy and the banking risks; second we notice the importance of new financial instruments concentrated in the principal centres; third the influence of operators on regulation; and finally the emergence of financial conglomerates and of cyber-money. The full-scale liberalization of trade may thus constitute an ideal environment for corruption and criminalization.

Two examples come to mind. The first concerns the end of the trade monopoly with China decided by the East India Company in 1834, which increased, as we have seen, opium smuggling destined for the Middle Empire, related to the very lively competition between negotiators and traffickers. The second, more recent, example concerns the emergence of Mafia practices in Wall Street. An investigation carried out by *Business Week* magazine analysed the network of four New Yorker 'families' and a group of Russian Mafia, which ran their enterprise on a part of the unlisted bonds market and in the Nasdaq electronic market. The panoply of interventions began with the manipulation of bonds through eviction, then the exploitation through legislation of foreign investments, in order to buy values at low prices from offshore centres, passing through the 'protection' offers of brokerage societies who were threatened by the stock markets offensives. Despite the complaints received from different victims of intimidation and of violence, the Securities and Exchange Commission carried out no investigations, due to a lack of proof on the illegality of the transactions. Such an attitude permits Mafia practices. As long as this manoeuvring is not denounced, as *Business Week* concluded on the American business environment, 'organized crime will continue to be the silent partner of financial markets.'[65]

If one admits, with regard to the tendencies of the international financial system, and to these examples, that corruption and criminalization are not necessarily related to the omnipresence of the State, but may also prosper in competitive market environments, qualified with an elaborated legal framework, the idea of treating these problems with a deregulation and liberalization rescue appears to be unrealistic. The examples of Tokyo, London and New York, the three principal financial centres of the world, have demonstrated to us that no power and no financial players, including the most competitive, are today safe from doubtful investments and from the corruption which protects them. At the political level, the Asiangate scandal revealed that the American Democratic Party was able to accept donations from Chinese economic leaders such as Wang Jun, chief executive of the China International Trade and Investment Corporation (CITIC), whose name was quoted in 1996 with that of general He Ping, son-in-law to Deng Xiaoping, in a dark AK 47 trafficking affair destined for the USA.

The British Conservative party received donations worth £1 million from the *Oriental Daily News* group, the biggest-circulation Hong Kong daily. The executive director of the press society, Ma Ching-kwan, clearly indicated that the deposit of funds before the retrocession of the territory to China, was related to the abandonment of local suits against his father, Ma Sik-chun, and his uncle, Ma Sik-yu, known as 'White powder Ma', one of the heroin trafficking godfathers who has found refuge in Taiwan since the 1970s. The Chairman of the Conservative party denied that this financing was the object of an illegal subcontracting; the last governor of Hong Kong, Chris Patten, denied all responsibility in the affair, and the Foreign Affairs Minister, Robin Cook, suggested finally that the money be used for drug rehabilitation programmes in Great Britain, instead of returning it to the Ma family, as had originally been proposed.[66]

The Japanese case has illustrated how a financial sector, dominating on a world scale, may be invested in and corrupted by organized crime. The recycling of mafia profits helped to divert the allocation of resources towards stock and real estate speculation. The financial system was destabilized and underwent a crisis that had a profound effect on the real economy. But this sequence of events is not specifically Japanese. The crises in Mexico (1994) and Thailand (1997), which then spread into Asia and throughout the emerging nations, are dramatic illustrations of the obscure relationships between criminalization and financial destabilization, in a massive laundering of narco-dollars.

Notes

1 Cf. Nahid Mohavedi, 'Les mutations du capitalisme japonais', in *Rapport moral sur l'argent dans le monde*, 1996, Financial Economic Association, Paris.

2 Cf. Christopher Wood, *The Bubble Economy: Japan's Extraordinary Speculation Boom of the 80's and the Dramatic Bust of the 90's*, New York, The Atlantic Monthly Press, 1992.

3 Cf. Vincent Renard, 'La corruption et l'immobilier au Japon', *Rapport moral sur l'argent dans le monde*, 1996, p. 61.

4 Cf. Malcom Trevor, 'The overseas strategies of Japanese corporations', *The Annals of the American Academy of Social Sciences*, no. 513, January 1991, p. 97.

5 Cf. Evelyne Dourille-Feer, *L'économie japonaise*, Editions La Découverte, collection Repères, Paris, 1998.

6 Cf. Thierry Ribault, 'Au Japon, la folie du "Pachinko"', *Le Monde diplomatique*, August, 1998; Nahid Mohavedi, 'Drogue et blanchiment au Japon', *Rapport moral sur l'argent dans le monde*, 1995, pp. 51–2; Thierry Cretin, *Mafias du monde*, PUF, 1997, p. 73.

7 Cf. Maki Murakami, 'Japan's drug war', *Look Japan*, February 1991; *International Herald Tribune*, 16 June 1992.

8 Cf. Vincent Renard, 'La corruption et l'immobilier au Japon', *Rapport moral sur l'argent dans le monde*, Paris, 1996.

9 Cf. Nahid Mohavedi, 'Crise et scandale dans l'immobilier japonais', *Rapport moral sur l'argent dans le monde*, 1995, Paris, Financial Economic Association, p. 230.

10 Cf. Philippe Pons, *Le Monde diplomatique*, May 1989.

11 Cf. Jean-Marie Bouissou, in Della Porta and Mény (eds), *Démocratie et corruption en Europe*, Paris, La Découverte, 1995.

12 Ibid.

13 Cf. *The Economist*, 26 September 1996.

14 Cf. *Financial Times*, 12 December 1995.

15 Cf. *International Herald Tribune*, 16 February 1996.

16 Dourille-Feer, *L'économie japonaise*, p. 59. On the debt estimation attributed to the *yakuza*, cf. *International Herald Tribune*, 16 February 1996.

17 Cf. *Business Week*, 29 January 1996, p. 16.

18 Cf. Christian Sautter, 'L'économie japonaise en mutation', *Politique étrangère*, Summer 1996, p. 307.

19 Dourille-Feer, *L'économie japonaise*, for the debt estimates at the end of 1995. The comparison with the Crédit Lyonnais is made by Christian Sautter, note 18. According to certain estimates, the stabilization of Crédit Lyonnais' debt represents an amount of FF150 billion (US$25 billion) for the French taxpayer (Cf. *Financial Times*, 2 March 1998).

20 Cf. *Business Week*, 29 January 1996, p. 15 and *Asia Week*, 3 May 1996, p. 52.

21 Cf. *Financial Times*, 13 January 1998; 14 January 1998.

22 Cf. *Business Week*, 29 January 1996, p. 15 and *Financial Times*, 12 December 1995, p. 8.

23 Cf. *International Herald Tribune*, 16 December 1996: 70 per cent of the US$65 billion of insolvent debts of the *jusen* is generally attributed to the *yakuza*, in other words US$45.5 billion.

24 Cf. *Asia Week*, 3 May 1996.

25 Dourille-Feer, *L'économie japonaise*, ch. 5.

26 Cf. Jongsoo Lee, 'The crisis of non-performing loans, a crisis for the Japanese financial system', *The Pacific Review*, 1997, no. 1, pp. 57–83.

27 Cf. *Financial Times*, 27 October 1997.

28 Cf. AFP Tokyo, 2 December 1997.

29 Cf. Schichihei Yamamoto, 'Japanese tradition and Japanese capitalism', *Japanese Economic Studies*, July–August 1994, quoted from Nahid Mohavedi, *Rapport moral sur l'argent dans le monde*, 1996, p. 124.

30 Cf. *Financial Times*, 26, 27 July 1997; *Far Eastern Economic Review*, 26 June 1997, pp. 63–4.

31 Cf. *Financial Times*, 18 September 1997, p. 17.

32 Cf. *Financial Times*, 24 October 1997.

33 Cf. *Financial Times*, 17 October 1997.

34 Cf. *Business Week*, 29 January 1996, p. 15.

35 Cf. Natacha Aveline, 'Japon: la gestion à hauts risques de la crise immobilière', *Etudes Foncières* no. 72, September 1996; Vincent Renard, 'La corruption et l'immobilier au Japon', *Rapport moral sur l'argent dans le monde*, 1996.

36 Cf. Philippe Pons, *Le Monde*, 18 February 1995, p. 24; *Financial Times*, 16–17 March 1996.

37 Cretin, *Mafias du monde*.

38 Cf. *International Herald Tribune*, 16 February 1996.

39 Cf. Philippe Pons, 'Banque et pègre nippones: les noces de plomb', *Le Monde*, 19 March 1996.

40 Ibid.

41 Cf. *Financial Times*, 26 November 1997; 1 December 1997, p. 17.

42 Cf. *Financial Times*, 4 February 1998; 11 February 1998.

43 CF. *Financial Times*, 31 January 1998; *Le Monde*, 1–2 February 1998.

44 Cf. *Japon Economie et Société*, no. 278, January 1998.

45 Cf. *Financial Times*, 13 February 1998, p. 7; *Far Eastern Economic Review*, 22 January 1998, p. 45.

46 Cf. *Financial Times*, 11 February 1998, p. 6; 26 February 1998, p. 6.

47 Cf. Brian Bremner, *Business Week*, 29 January 1996.

48 Bouissou, *Démocratie et corruption*, pp. 131–43.

49 Mohavedi, 'Crise et scandales', p. 231.

50 Bouissou, in *Democratie et corruption*.

51 Cf. Kyodo News Service, 23 December 1997 in SWB BBC Asia-Pacific, 24 December 1997; *China Daily*, 21 February 1998.

52 Cf. *Le Monde*, 13 October 1992.

53 Cf. for example the interview with Christian Sautter, 'Le Japon engagé dans la démolition d'un "oligopole cordial"', *Revue*

d'économie financière, The Japanese financial system, no. 43, October 1997.

54 Except Michel Aglietta, who insisted on 'the long delays of awareness and maturation of the problems', attributed according to him to 'the Japanese method of searching for compromise.' Cf. 'La réforme du système financier Japonais', *Revue d'économie financière*, no. 43, October 1997.

55 Cf. *Le Monde*, 16 June 1994 and 17 June 1994, p. 13.

56 Mohavedi, 'Les mutations du capitalisme japonais'.

57 Cf. Michel Aglietta, 'La crise bancaire en France et dans le monde', *La lettre du CEPII*, March 1997.

58 Cf. Thomas Lambert, Jacques Le Cacheux and Audrey Mahuet, 'L'épidémie de crises bancaires dans les pays de l'OECD', *Revue de l'OFCE*, April 1997.

59 Cf. Christian Chavagneux and Eric Nicolas, 'L'influence des acteurs privés sur la régulation financière internationale', *Politique étrangère*, no. 3, 1997.

60 Cf. Laurence Scialom, 'Les conglomérats financiers, un défi prudentiel', *Revue d'économie financière*: Reflections on the French Banking system, no. 39, February 1997.

61 Cf. Philippe Chalmin, *Cyclope*, The World Markets, 1996, Ed. Economica, Paris.

62 Cf. IMF Bulletin, 18 September 1995.

63 Cf. Jean de Maillard, *Un monde sans loi, la criminalité financière en images*, Paris, Ed. Stock, 1998.

64 Cf. Romeo Ciminello, 'Drogue et produits financiers dérivés', *Rapport moral sur l'argent dans le monde*, 1995, Financial Economy Association, pp. 113–17.

65 Cf. *Business Week*, 16 December 1996, pp. 50–8.

66 Cf. *Financial Times*, 21 January 1998; Alfred MacCoy, *La politique de l'héroine en Asie du Sud-Est*, Paris, Flammarion, 1980; *Pingguo ribao* (Apple daily) Hong Kong, 20 January 1998, in SWB BBC Asia-Pacific, 24 January 1998; Radio TV Hong Kong, 21 January 1998, in SWB BBC Asia-Pacific, 23 January 1998.

5

Crisis and Laundering in Mexico: From the 'Tequila Effect' to the 'Cocaine Effect'

———◆———

What happened in Japan, on the basis of a trade surplus of commercial balances in the 1980s and which provoked an over-liquidity of the economy and of credit facilities, was reproduced in developing countries such as Mexico and Thailand, on the basis of short-term flows of portfolio investments. According to the US State Department, these two countries, which had similar trade liberalization and privatization policies, had become, just before their financial crises, the principal narco-dollars recycling centres in the western and eastern hemispheres.[1]

In the case of Mexico, the Attorney General of the Republic estimated that the local cartel benefit from recycled drugs money in the economy from 1984 to 1994 represented US$30 billion, or 10 per cent of GDP at the end of the period.[2] Other experts such as Charles Intriago, the editor of *Money Laundering Alert*, estimate that the laundering carried out by the Mexican cartels, which control one-third of the American market for illegal drugs, worth US$50 billion, may reach US$8 billion per year.[3] American officials are more explicit: 75 per cent of the cocaine and half of the cannabis consumed in the USA comes from Mexico, and the local drug cartels gain an annual profit of US$10–30 billion.[4] This estimation is plausible with regard to the profits of criminal organizations, but needs to be treated with caution when it comes to their nationality.

The cocaine and crack market, which represents 9 million American consumers as opposed to 1 million heroin addicts and 20 million cannabis smokers, generates a turnover of US$40 billion per year, according to the estimations of Peter Reuter, one of the most respected experts on the subject.[5] The Rand Drug Policy Research Centre estimates that criminal organizations make a net profit equivalent to 75 per cent of the particular sale of cocaine, or US$30 billion per year.[6] If 75 per cent of the American market is delivered by the Mexicans, the cartels of this country would gain annual profits of US$22.5 billion, by controlling the retail distribution. It remains to be seen whether the Mexican cartels do in fact control distribution. An adviser to President Ernesto Zedillo made this comment to journalist Andres Oppenheimer:

> 'you keep talking about the Mexican drug cartels, but what about the U.S. drug cartels ? Are you going to tell me that there is a thirty-billion-dollar drug smuggling business into the United States and that there aren't any Mafia bosses handling that business on your side of the border?'[7]

Apart from this objection, which highlights the share of responsibility of the two countries, it is incontestable that Mexico has become an important place for transiting, providing and laundering for the biggest drug market of the world. This invisible transition accelerated by the North American Free Trade Agreement (NAFTA) and the anti-laundering legislation reinforcement in the USA, heavily and durably marks the Mexican economy, society and politics. In the 1980s, most of the Columbian cocaine was transited via Central America and the Caribbean on tourist planes, most often the Cessnas. According to the US anti-drug services, the Mexicans took a 10–15 per cent commission for their various services, such as the availability of numerous private landing runways in their country, transshipment and the distribution of the merchandise in the USA.[8]

As of the end of the 1980s, when the border between the USA and Mexico superseded Florida as the principal entry point of drugs to the American market, the Mexican cartels increased their commission to 40–50 per cent of the value of the load, or set up their own accounts by buying, with cash, Columbian cocaine stocks, whose transportation they assured as well as an undetermined proportion of the distribution by creating their own networks in the USA. The presence of 3–4 million non-regularized Mexican immigrants on American territory, and the annual flow of many hundreds of thousands of illegal immigrants, half of whom have installed themselves in California, facilitate this process.

This upstream and downstream strategy to control channels allows the Mexican cartels to take a significant slice of the added value, without doubt less than 75 per cent of the retail price, which would imply a total control of the distribution, but more likely around 50 per cent. On this low estimate with regard to other evaluations,[9] the Mexicans would make US$15 billion of profits annually solely in the American market, to which it is necessary to add 4000 tons of cultivated and exported marijuana from 'emerald zones' from the north of the country and the 6 tons of heroin manufactured each year.[10] The annual narco-profit estimate of US$10–30 billion and US$3–8 billion from laundering therefore seems reasonable (this former amount being more realistic as of the 1990s). This simple calculation questions an idea that is generally accepted, according to which 90 per cent of the drug profits created in the Andean countries would be laundered in the USA.[11] It would be more correct to say 'from the United States'.

In fact, as of the 1990s, the evidence indicates that the Mexican criminal organizations have passed from a service provider status, to directors and launderers. This transition from artisan stage to industrial stage is illustrated by the replacement of the Cessnas by old Boeing 727s or DC 7s, sometimes transporting cargoes of more than 10 tons of cocaine from Columbia to Mexico, before the transshipment of the merchandise to the USA.[12] The recycling of narco-profits simultaneously reaches significant proportions at the macro-economic level, by mobilizing small business, the real estate sector, and, on a larger scale, local financial inter-mediation.

Laundering helps to create a grey market of foreign exchange and bonds, where the agents and the stockbrokers take a commission of 10–15 per cent for their services.[13] Commercial transactions are also used, where more than 70 per cent of the foreign trade of Mexico is with the USA. The USA derives an indirect advantage from the recycling, as it increases its export opportunities by allowing certain Mexican businessmen to import American goods and services paid for with their narco-profits.[14] It is by definition difficult to measure the impact of this situation on foreign trade. The day before the crisis, the annual laundered funds, US$3–8 billion, were comparable to petroleum exports (US$6.7 billion). They represent 4–10 per cent of the total Mexican imports (US$80 billion in 1994) and 5–15 per cent of the imports coming from the USA (US$55 billion in 1994), but not all the profit is laundered through foreign trade. We may nevertheless affirm that the drug money facilitates the purchase of American consumption goods, automobiles or electronics, where the manufactured products represent 65 per cent of the Mexican imports. In a country where domestic savings are traditionally low, these consumption facilities are operated to the detriment of investment, and of the balance of trade. Far from reducing the annual servicing of the foreign debt, which represented US$13–16 billion from 1993 to 1995, drug money contributed to increasing a dependence on imports, thus deteriorating the current balance.

The dynamic of investment is itself deeply marked by the privatization policies which have intensified since 1991, by integrating the banking sector, the services and the infra-structure. The privatization of more than 900 Mexican

enterprises, estimated at US$26 billion, allowed an ameliora-
tion of the state of the public finances, but numerous gaps
have appeared in the implementation process: according to
the OECD, they concern the feasibility studies, the
insufficiency of the regulatory framework, the confusion
between operators and evaluators, the lack of transparency in
the financial arrangements, or the excessive implication of the
State as guarantee for the profitability of the projects.[15]
Privatization blends with deregulation. Having authorized
private operators to construct and manage their own
harbours, in 1991, the government authorized the free
circulation of heavy lorries in all of the cities, harbours and
train stations. Authorised lorries increased by 62 per cent in
two years.[16]

In the area of infrastructure, between 1988 and 1994, 5800
km of toll freeways were created as a concession at the price
of US$15 billion, representing 43 per cent of the investment
needs for the period 1993–2000. The managers expect to
regain their investments as quickly as possible with the fear of
obtaining only short-term financing. This desire for rapid
profits on long-term projects is passed on to the toll fees,
which are on average five to six times higher than in the USA
for similar distances, prior to the 1995 crisis. Penalized by
surcharges, truckers prefer to use the free access roads, which
deteriorate quickly, thus increasing the State charged maintenance fees.[17]

These favourable privatization conditions, within the
framework of the liberalization of the North American
NAFTA market from January 1994, and Mexican membership
of the OECD, encourage the flow of essentially short-term
foreign capital to these operations through the intermediary
of banks and bond markets. The amelioration of 'funda-
mentals' of the economy, with the decrease of the budget
deficit,[18] and of inflation, which has fallen from 100 per cent
in 1988 to 10 per cent in 1994, contributes to this keen interest
in Mexico, presented as a model to the liberal orthodoxy
proposed by international sponsors for developing countries.

And yet, with regard to development, the performance of Mexico is a long way from that of the dragons and tigers of East Asia. From 1985 to 1995, real GDP increased, as an annual average, by only 2 per cent and the GDP per person by 0.1 per cent: the 'Mexican miracle' in fact hides a stagnating situation. But international financial companies are motivated by the very strong interest rate differentials between countries in the northern and southern hemispheres. With interest rates in the US dropping since 1990, the high interest rates maintained in Mexico and some Latin American countries have attracted financial capital that is disconnected from domestic production and unlikely to improve local competitiveness. From 1989 to 1994, portfolio investments reached US$70 billion and represented 72 per cent of the capital flow towards Mexico.[19] In 1993, the country received US$5 billion from direct foreign investments, an amount higher than the whole Eastern bloc in transition, and emitted the equivalent of US$28 billion in securities and Treasury bonds indexed on the US dollar, which represents a quarter of the portfolio investments destined for all of the Southern countries. The massive flow of these currency funds favours the appreciation of the peso, the fall of export competitiveness and the further increase of the current deficit, which reached 8 per cent of GDP in 1994.

The over-liquidity of the economy facilitated speculative investments in real estate, and an increase in stock values and household consumption, which decreased domestic savings from 21 to 11 per cent of GDP between 1989 and 1994. From 1987 to 1994, the volume of credit banking in the economy increased by 107 per cent in actual terms, and the household credit, in terms of housing or consumption by credit card, increased by 742 per cent.[20] The Mexican middle classes, the principal supporters of the Institutional Revolutionary Party in power, have been created on the basis of a 6 per cent growth from 1940 to 1980.[21] However, their access to the society of consumption, in the American style, announced during the rule of President Carlos Salinas, stems from an illusion of indebtedness: they take advantage of the deflation introduced by the competition of American products and of the imported savings introduced by the capital markets, making the credits accessible in US dollars.

Simultaneously, the gap widens between the 40 million poor people, in a total population of 90 million, and the small rich minority, who construct landing runways on their country properties.[22] The concentration of wealth reached previously unheard of dimensions, when the 13 Mexican billionaires identified in the greatest fortunes list according to *Forbes* magazine, were shown to own more than 10 per cent of the country's GDP.[23] In the great North American market euphoria and the high risk investments of 1994, the amount of the expired debt due to non-residents reached US$60 billion. The operators tend to be indebted in US dollars because of costly credits in pesos, but their profits are paid in pesos as well. As a result, they have built up exchange reserves to protect against an eventual depreciation of the peso which would increase their debts and import bills. The authorities defend the pegging of the peso to the dollar by eating into the exchange reserves, which slipped from US$28 billion at the end of 1993 to US$10 billion at the end of 1994. The 15 per cent depreciation of the peso, which finally occurred on 20 December, at the initiative of the new President Zedillo, caused a crisis of confidence among the investors, who withdrew their short-term capital, thereby worsening the collapse of the peso. The stabilization plan put into place by the IMF, worth US$50 billion, was matched by draconian budgetary conditions and the management of inflation, which was fully respected. Following a contraction of 6.2 per cent in the GDP and an unemployment rate of 7.6 per cent in 1995, 1996 saw a net recovery. GDP increased by 5.1 per cent; the budgetary balance was re-established; inflation decreased by 52 per cent in 1995 and by 27 per cent in 1996; and the rate of unemployment decreased by 4.1 per cent. Export competi- tiveness even allowed a proportion of the contracted debt with the United States and the IMF to be reimbursed.

Behind this reassuring recovery scenario, apart from commercial transactions and real estate investments, is hidden, in fact, a heavy privatization track record, which served as a true Trojan horse for the narco-traffickers. One of the most spectacular cases, revealed by the *Washington Post*,[24] is that of the National Company of popular support (Conasupo) which was quickly privatized under the rule of President Carlos Salinas (1988–94). This company, which controlled an important network of foodstuff distribution stores subsidised for poor families, was used by the President's brother, Raul Salinas, and many high-ranking civil servants, to channel cocaine to the USA and recycle the narco-profits on their bank accounts. This true take-over bid was apparently carried out to the benefit of the Gulf cartel led by Juan Garcia Abrego, who spent, according to his testimony, about US$50 million per month to corrupt the justice system, the police and the anti-drug forces under the leadership of Carlos Salinas.[25]

The privatization of transport infrastructure, roads, harbours and banks, provides further illustration of the dynamic of criminal investments: the circulation of the merchandise was facilitated with a minimum control, whereas the weakness or the absence of regulation on cash deposits in the Mexican financial system, and contemporary reinforcement of the American anti-laundering legislation on the other side of the border, reinforced the local recycling of narco-dollars.[26] The penetration of banks and regional exchange agencies by narco-capital has caused rumours since the beginning of the leadership of President Carlos Salinas de Gortari:[27] in 1991, the private sector bought out for the sum of US$12 billion, or three times the accounting value, 18 large banks which had been nationalized nine years earlier.[28] Businessmen with 'unexplainable fortunes', a euphemism which generally designates drug trafficking, were ready to purchase banks 'at loss'. Such is the case of Carlos Cabal Peniche, who bought up the Union Bank at two or three times its value, before taking control of Fresh Del Monte

Produce, a large distribution chain of agricultural products. The same source generously feeds the chests of the Institutional Revolutionary Party, which has been in power for 70 years.[29] This example, which was subject to a judicial case, is not the only one: most of the privatizations, linked with or related to drug money have been neither detected nor questioned.[30]

Gradual investment in banks and stocks has been the driving force behind the economic ascent of the drug traffickers, much to the detriment of the legal sectors: access to credit and to international financing allows the practice of laundering to be institutionalised by increasing narco-profits. The annual recycling of US$3–8 billion of drug money represented only 1–3 per cent of GDP in 1994, but the accumulation of these money flows, a dozen years later, represented 10–25 per cent of GDP. If the proportion of these funds destined for consumption, by feeding imports of manufactured products from the USA, is taken away, the available proportion for investment has a not insignificant economic impact. The increase of investment opportunities and credits will thus increase the economic and political influence of narco-traffickers. We have seen the numerous irregularities which have accompanied the transfer of public assets. The privatization of Telmex, for example, the Mexican telephone monopoly, in co-ordination with France Télécom, allowed for a rise in fees of 247 per cent. This was so heavily criticized by clients that the company had to change to a simple increase of 170 per cent.[31]

In the case of Telmex and for certain banks, privatization, primarily profiting from the Public Treasury, poses the same questions. The first concerns the identity of the new owners: 'when you sell in haste, you do not truly know who the buyer is', as stated by Jorge Castaneda.[32] The second concerns the concession granted by the political power in exchange for high asset prices. It may be the authorization of high price increases, in the new framework of NAFTA, which allowed monopolies to be acquired by the principal Mexican enterprises, controlled by the 13 largest, wealthiest families. That was the case for Don Emilio Azcarraga's Television group, which reaches 90 per cent of the Mexican audience, or for Roberto Hernandez's Banamex bank group, both of which are protected from foreign competition for 12–15 years from 1994. The new alliance sealed between the political power and business groups under the leadership of Carlos Salinas also has its obligations. Each large group was invited to contribute US$25 million to the election campaign of the Institutional Revolutionary Party in 1994, which cost the enormous amount of US$700 million.[33]

This national level investment works just as well as at regional level through government intermediaries, as shown through the work of Jean Rivelois.[34] The forced contributions of the legal entrepreneurs, just like narco-traffickers, serve to feed the clientele system of the IRP, the financing of the party in power, the enrichment of the political class and social redistribution programmes such as Solidarity and Procampo. In this sense, narco-trafficking and profit laundering take place in the institutional arena. According to Jean Rivelois, this is not a matter of social peripheries infiltrating the centre of power, but rather of the centre annexing or instrumentalizing the peripheries. The recycling dynamic was thus able to feed the tourist investments in Cancun, and in Acapulco, under the governance of José Francisco Ruiz Massieu, or the harbour investments in Manzanillo, under the leadership of Miguel de la Madrid, President of the Republic from 1982 to 1988. In this last case, the Sinaloa cartel was implicated, in liaison with that of Guadalajara, one of the two Mexican drug capitals, with the border city of Tijuana, in the south of California.

These field observations suggest links between certain hypotheses concerning the murders of Cardinal Posadas (1993), of the 1994 IRP presidential campaign candidate, Colosio, and of the IRP General Secretary, Ruiz Massieu, who had plunged the country into its worst political crisis since the 1920s, before the monetary and economic shock of

1995. According to Jorge Castaneda, one of the most respected analysts of the Mexican political system, it is conceivable that Carlos Salinas' regime was able to reach an agreement with narco-traffickers as of 1988. The most modern factions of the drug barons would have been authorized to discreetly carry on their activities on the national territory, on the condition that they avoid all interference in relations with the USA and locally launder their profits. This would lead to a drop in the current account deficit, as shown by the Colombian experience in the 1980s. The nomination of an Attorney General and a drug czar, who were both well-known to drug traffickers, along with the persistent rumours about the recycling of narco-profits in the privatizations, support this hypothesis. However, the USA would have increased its pressure following the growth of trafficking, causing a breakdown of the tacit agreement. The assassinations of the Cardinal and of the two principal politicians in the country would thus be interpreted as a warning from the gangsters for the government to stop their repression.

The end of the traditional methods of conflict regulation among the elite was due to the increasingly invasive presence of the drug traffickers, who, after having joined forces with the most efficient and most wealthy regional businessmen, could manipulate the political and industrial parties so as to obtain their objectives. Jorge Castaneda goes beyond a simple integration and instrumentalization of the social margin by the Centre: 'it is not inconceivable', he writes, 'that at the high trafficking level, the distinction between politicians who have become drug barons, or the drug barons who have become politicians, [has] become very delicate'.[35] While waiting, perhaps for a long time, for the results of judicial investigations, these speculations may be pushed a long way. It is possible that scores are settled through murders, and that these crimes, far from being the product of IRP dinosaur conspiracies against economic liberalization – a theory defended by former President Carlos Salinas – are related to the share of narco-profits withdrawn at the regional level.

Other Latin-American examples show the extent of the complicity between politics, the business circle and the narco-trafficking. In Columbia, the country where 80 per cent of the world extraction of emeralds takes place, Victor Carranza, a major producer and exporter, was arrested, accused of cocaine trafficking, laundering and homicides. This dollar billionaire, on the list of the most wealthy in *Forbes* magazine, actively contributed to the financing of the government in power.[36] The Japanese case, on the other hand, illustrates the length of the legal procedures which have allowed relations to become established between the business circle and the criminal underworld since the 1980s. If it was necessary to wait until 1997 to start making some changes in Mexico, what must we think of the Mexican procedures, in a country where the independence of justice is one of the objectives of president Ernest Zedillo (1994–2000)? The arrest of Raul Salinas, brother of Carlos Salinas, accused of the murder of Jose Francisco Ruiz Massieu, and the escape of former President Salinas to Ireland prove the determination of the investigators, but certain signs mark the persistence of the Mexican crisis.

The police moved beyond simple corruption to enter into the world of full-fledged criminality. Half of the 900 armed gangs registered in the country are composed of active or retired army forces. It is no longer possible to count the huge number of embezzlements of the drug seizures, nor the incidents between the various police forces, who may sometimes even serve as body guards for traffickers. Some officials estimate that half of the Federal Police agents make a profit from drug trafficking, either by bribing, or by stealing a proportion of the cocaine. At State level, the police forces, even the lower paid, succumb to pressure from the drug barons, to such an extent that many among them are only 'crime unions in uniform', an expression coined by Andres Oppenheimer, resorting to kidnapping for ransom in hard times. The current use of parallel police forces in civil uniforms, the *madrinas* or *godmothers*, who have unattractive responsibilities, such as the assassination of opposition activists, contributes to the confusion between policemen and thieves, policemen and assassins. This reached devastating dimensions during the economic recession in 1995. The corruption is orchestrated by the hierarchy, the higher ranks of the police or by the anti-drug force who generally make fortunes in their functions. From 1993 to 1995, 10 per cent of the federal judicial police were fired for having had relations with the drug cartels.[37] In February 1997, General Jesus Gutiérrez Rebollo, director of the National Institute for the fight against drug trafficking (INCD), was arrested for collusion with the cartels of Tijuana and of Juarez, and 1200 agents of his organizations were fired. These political decisions do not greatly reduce the rewards of the narco-traffickers, who are the principal source of corruption.

The police, judiciary, small business circles or high administration are not the only ones concerned, as shown by the example of the Grupo Financiero Anahuac, a small Mexican bank acquired in 1995 by the Juarez cartel, the major criminal organization of the country. The investigation of prosecutor Salvatti has shown the laundering mechanisms which used people related to political or union leaders of the IRP, who were socially well-known. The Anahuac group thus recruited the son and the nephew of former President of the Republic, Miguel de la Madrid, and tried to implicate President Zedillo's brother, Rodolofo Zedillio, an architect working on a hotel project worth US$50 million and situated right in the middle of the financial district of the capital.[38]

In economic matters, the return of growth may give the illusion that the problems have disappeared. It is a little early to forget that the foreign debt reached US$160 billion, condemning the country to export at the expense of domestic demand and of better distribution of internal incomes. But the return of growth also hides another problem, just as serious: the domestic debt related to bank liabilities. We have seen that the banks and the brokerage companies have channelled 72 per cent of the foreign investments to Mexico between 1989 and 1994, in other words US$70 billion. In this expansion phase, which corresponds to the period of privatization, the Mexican financial system derived considerable profits by exercising intermediation margins (the difference between deposit rates and savings rates) which are among the highest in the world. Banking has become a much more profitable activity than production investments, favouring the involvement of large American or Spanish establishments on the local market.[39]

Consumer credit items (automobiles, houses), the mainly financial valorization of capital or the development of large tourist, real estate or infrastructure projects conceived for very short terms, twist the allocation of resources at the expense of the productive sector, thus increasing imports and creating overcapacity with regard to domestic demand. The 1995 crisis brutally changed the data: the reduction or withdrawal of portfolio capital, and the collapse of the currency, doubled the value of peso credits fixed in dollars, which were more valuable before the devaluation. The number of insolvent debtors, households and enterprises, increases, while overcapacity in real estate and tourism rise accentuated by the recession. To avoid the collapse of the financial system, the State is forced to help the rescheduling of household and enterprise credits, and to re-purchase portfolios of bad bank debts, in exchange for re-capitalization by their stockbrokers or by investors. The entire rescue measure is evaluated at US$45 billion, equivalent to three-quarters of the total bank loans in 1988 and 14 per cent of GDP in 1996.[40]

If this aid, spread over a period of a dozen years, may be painless, it resorts to the same logic of collectivization of the losses that we have seen in the Japanese case. There is a difference, nevertheless, of size: the proceeds of privatization had brought US$26 billion to the Mexican State, US$12 billion of which were solely for the banks, allowing a stabilization of public finances. Today the figure is four times higher – which public leaders have to disburse, affecting the majority of taxpayers, in order to cover the hazardous operations of privatized groups or imported credit consumption from the middle and upper classes. The excesses of the bank sector and the crisis which followed it were balanced not only by collectivizing these losses but also by privatizing the potential beneficiaries; the privatization of the banks was assessed, after the crisis, at US$37 billion in the State accounts (US$45 billion of bad debts taken into control minus US$12 billion bank asset transfers). The Mexican bankers then invented a new formula, that of a subsidized privatization, which allows the State to give away its assets by *paying* the new owners an amount equivalent to 10 per cent of the GDP in 1996.

The responsibility of the different operators in the exorbitant cost of the financial crisis remains to be established. The essentially American portfolio investments, which were attracted by the high interest rates allowing a quick valorization of capital, were cooled down by the accentuation of the political crisis and the devalorization of the peso, threatening the reimbursement of their investments. The IMF and the United States' rescue plan (US$50 billion) allowed a retrieval of their investment risks at the expense of the Mexican taxpayers, but its absence would have been even more damaging by launching a series of failures of banking establishments incapable of reimbursing their foreign debt. The scarcity of credit and the economic recession would have been much more serious than that of 1995, not to mention the consequences for other Latin American countries and the emerging markets.[41] Definitely, the responsibility of the local financial intermediaries appears to have been just as decisive: domestic savings, in the same way as the imported savings, had been affected by short-term speculative projects, including some in the area of infrastructure, where the risks were thereafter taken up by public leaders.

Apart from this co-responsibility, which does not excuse the ambiguous game played by the US, the question that we must analyse is the impact of the recycling on the criminal capital in the financial system and the allocation of resources. The multiplication of political-financial scandals under the leadership of Ernesto Zedillio, and the impunity they enjoyed, are just as much symptomatic of the mysterious relationships that have been formed, and even reinforced, among the centres of power, financial circles and drug trade under the Salinas era. Jorge Lankenau, former president of the Banca Confia and one of the most important businessmen in the city of Monterrey, in the State of Nuevo Leon, is the third banker to escape arrest since the crisis of 1994, after having been sentenced to three months' house arrest in his home worth US$20 million. The irregular operations of the Banca Confia, which has been re-capitalized by the State for US$1 billion, concern suspect transactions with a stockbroker subsidiary and offshore companies, an aggressive market strategy and certain real estate investments.[42]

Without prejudice to the investigation results, and in a similar fashion to other financial affairs we have discussed, all the laundering ingredients can be seen here: offshore companies, high-risk real estate investment and unfair competition. This last point emphasizes the contagious recycling effects on the financial system. If it is reasonable to think that about one-quarter of the funds laundered annually (in other words, 750 million to 2 billion US$) were invested in the Mexican banking sector over a period of ten years, this would yield a figure of 7.5 to 20 billion US$, without considering the actual interest rates, which is to say, 8 to 22 per cent of total bank credits at the end of 1997. Most of the time, these funds are invested in regional or new establishments, whose activities are less easy to trace than those of larger groups. Certain economists look into the origin of the banking crisis in Latin America without explaining narco-profit problems, and interpret it as 'a spoiled fruit which may rot the entire basket':[43] in the new environment of financial deregulation, the competition that the banks experienced in remunerating savings may have become a disadvantage to most competitive enterprises. A 'bad' bank proceeding with risky investments tends to remunerate the deposits at a higher rate than a 'good' bank. Its more aggressive attitude will allow it to win some of the clientele from other establishments, reassured by the existence of insurance on its deposits, and eventually to intervene in the inter-bank market. The 'good' banks then find themselves faced with a dilemma between the decrease in volume of their activity or adopting a risky loan strategy, allowing them to align themselves with the remuneration of savings as practised by their competitors. Whatever the choice made, the result is the same: 'the bank portfolios which adopt a risky loan policy will increase to the detriment of more conservative banks, and the entire financial system will then be more fragile.'[44] The recycling of narco-profits in the bank sector, initially involving relatively limited funds, may thus increase with the accumulation of black money flows, and subsequently weaken the entire financial system through unfair competition.

The Casablanca operation, which mobilized 200 American agents of the customs service and the FBI, greatly supported this hypothesis. Following a three-year investigation, the longest on laundering in the history of the USA, the American services arrested, in May 1998 at San Diego (California) and at Las Vegas (Nevada), 25 high-ranking Mexican executives from 12 of the 19 principal banks in Mexico. Most of the accused worked in two drug capitals, Tijuana, on the border with the USA, and the region of Guadalajara. Three banks were directly implicated in the cartels' money laundering, involving a total of 112 suspects: Bancomer, the pre-eminent Mexican banking establishment, Serfin, the third and most important, and Banca Confia. Other groups such as Banacci, the second bank of Mexico, Banamex, and the subsidiaries of the two Spanish companies, Santander and Bilbao-Bizcaya, have been equally mentioned but without being accused. The opposition deputies asked for the resignation of the governor of the Central Bank, Guillermo Ortiz, for its role in the privatization of the banking system, in 1991–92: 'the privatization and the permissive supervision transformed Mexico into a laundering paradise', declared Doloris Padierna in front of the National Assembly. For the president of the Mexican Bank Association, the Casablanca operation is not proof that the financial system has been penetrated by drugs-trafficking, to the extent that the majority of the important funds recycled by a Mexican bank did not surpass US$20 million. We have already found the justice in this argument.[45]

The laundering dimension thus allows us to realize the shortcomings of local financial intermediation, which has played an important role in the Mexican crisis. At this stage of our analysis, the error would be to overestimate its impact, by making it the determining element of unbalance: this would theoretically have arisen in its absence. The liberalization of trade, the volatility of the portfolio investments are by nature exogenous factors, independent of recycling; the local speculative tendencies existed prior to the economic influence of the drugs trade. Nevertheless, in practice, strong links were developed between these phenomena and the expansion of narco-trafficking, to such an extent that a quasi-symbiotic relationship seems to have been created between the legal and illegal spheres. By voluntarily limiting our analysis to drug trafficking, we have put aside all other lucrative activities such as illegal immigration to the USA, which involves hundreds of thousands of people each year. The laundering dimension thus seems to have been underestimated, and deserves to be examined further in other field studies. But its impact remains significant, even by examining only a minimum of data. In the economic domain, laundering has essentially increased imports of American consumer goods, and, by penetrating the bank sector, it has greatly contributed – through the unequal competition – to diverting the allocation of resources towards unproductive net import sectors.

What has been called the 'tequila effect', this artificial prosperity, constructed on indebtedness and imports without a significant increase of economic competitiveness, is thus inextricably related to the 'cocaine effect'. This devastating cocktail not only provoked the crisis of 1994–95, but also launched the implosion of the IRP, the great disintegration of the police and justice, not to mention the development of gangsterism. The impact of laundering may also be shown in the case of Thailand, which served as a catalyst for the Asian crisis, as of July 1997.

Notes

1 Cf. International Narcotics Control Strategy Report, 1996, US Department of State.

2 Cretin, *Mafias du monde*, p. 11.

3 Cf. *Financial Times*, 25 March 1998, p. 6.

4 Cf. Andres Oppenheimer, *Bordering on Chaos: Guerrillas, Stockbrokers, Politicians and Mexico's Road to Prosperity*, Boston, Little Brown 1996, p. 164.

5 Cf. Peter Reuter, 'The export demand for Latin American drugs', North South Center, University of Miami, March 1995, quoted in Francesco Thoumi, 'Pays andins: l'échec des politiques anti-drogue', *Problèmes d'Amérique Latine* no. 188, July–September 1995.

6 Cf. Marie Christine Dupuis, *Stupéfiants, prix, profits: l'économie politique du marché des stupéfiants industriels*, PUF 1996, p. 207.

7 Oppenheimer, *Bordering on Chaos*, p. 312.

8 Cf. Francesco Thoumi, '*Pays andins*', p. 11.

9 Dupuis, *Stupéfiants* pp. 206 and 218.

10 Cf. *US News and World Report*, 29 January 1996 quoted in Cretin, *Mafias du monde*.

11 Thoumi, '*Pays andins*', p. 15.

12 Oppenheimer, *Bordering on Chaos*, p. 164.

13 Cf. INCSR, US Department of State, 1996.

14 Ibid.

15 Cf. *Developpement régional et politiques structurelles au Mexique*, OECD, 1998, pp. 110–30.

16 Cf. Paul Stare, *Global Habit*, 1997, p. 56.

17 Cf. OECD, *Developpement régional*, p. 123.

18 The reduction of the budgetary deficit is related to the privatization policy, which has considerably diminished the number of State

enterprises, from 1155 in 1982 to 160 in 1993. These sales brought the equivalent of US$26–27 billion to the Public Treasury. Cf. OECD, *Developpement régional*, p. 116.

19 Cf. Robert Rollinat, 'Anatomie d'une crise financière', *Problèmes d'Amèrique Latine*, no. 21, June 1996.

20 Cf. Christophe Cordonnier, 'Mexique: au delà de la reprise, vers le modèle chilien', *Problèmes d'Amérique Latine*, no. 22, July–September 1996, p. 9.

21 Cf. Jorge Castaneda, *The Mexican Shock: its Meaning for the US*, New York, The New Press, 1996, p. 45.

22 Cf. John Whitehead and Marie-Josée Kravis, 'Lessons of the Mexican Peso Crisis', Independent Task Force, Council on Foreign Relations, Washington, p. 45: unpublished, quoted in Alma Guillermoprieto, 'Mexico: Murder without justice', *New York Review of Books*, 3 October 1996.

23 Castaneda, *The Mexican Shock*, p. 216.

24 Cf. *Washington Post*, 11 May 1997 quoted in *Le Monde*, 17 May 1997.

25 Cf. *Money Laundering Alert*, quoted in *La Dépêche internationale des drogues*, DGO, Paris, January 1997, no. 63.

26 Cf. INCSR, US Department of State, 1996.

27 Castaneda, *The Mexican Shock*, p. 167.

28 Cf. Alain Musset, *Le Mexique*, Paris, Editions. Armand Colin, 1996, p. 168.

29 Whitehead and Kravis, 'Lessons of the Mexican Peso Crisis'.

30 Castaneda, *The Mexican Shock*, p. 246.

31 Oppenheimer, *Bordering on Chaos*, p. 92.

32 Castaneda, *The Mexican Shock*, p. 185.

33 Oppenheimer, *Bordering on Chaos*, chapter: The Banquet.

34 Cf. Jean Rivelois, *Drogues et pouvoirs: du Mexique au paradis*, Ed. L'Harmattan, Paris, 1999.

35 Castaneda, *The Mexican Shock*, p. 170 and ch. 9.

36 Cf. *La Dépêche internationale des drogues*, no. 78, April 1998, Drug Geopolitics Observatory, Paris.

37 Cf. On these statistics Oppenheimer, *Bordering on Chaos*, ch. 15: The police connection.

38 Cf. *Financial Times*, 25 March 1998.

39 Rollinat, 'Anatomie d'une crise financière', p. 108.

40 Cf. *Financial Times*, 5 November 1997.

41 This point of view is developed by Michel Aglietta, 'Défaillance des marchés et risques systémiques', *Revue d'économie financière*, Summer 1996.

42 Cf. *Financial Times*, 27 October 1997.

43 Cf. Michael Gavin and Ricardo Haussman, Interamercian Development Bank, 'Les origines des crises bancaires: le contexte macro-économique', *Problèmes d'Amérique Latine* no. 21, April–June 1996, p. 141.
44 Ibid.
45 Cf. *Financial Times*, 20 May 1998; *Le Monde*, 22 May 1998.

6

Crisis and Laundering in Thailand: The Provincial Godfathers' Launch on Bangkok

According to a study published by the great Thai specialist on corruption, Sungsidh Piriyarangsan, from Chulalongkorn University, laundering has reached major dimensions in the economy of Thailand. Six illegal activities, namely prostitution, gun running, smuggling of hydrocarbons, illegal gambling and trafficking in labour and drugs, produce the equivalent of 11–18 billion US$ annually, or 8–13 per cent of the GDP from 1993 to 1995. The most creative sector for parallel jobs is illegal gambling, involving four million people and about eight per cent of the GDP. Prostitution involves between 150 000 and 200 000 women, and produces at least four billion dollars annually, or two per cent of the GDP. By comparison, the overall drug traffic represents scarcely more than one billion dollars.[1] This figure is no doubt underestimated, since it concerns only the domestic market (comprised of 200 000 heroin addicts, 250 000 amphetamine users, and over 300 000 marijuana users) and wholesale heroin exports. The work of Sungsidh Piriyarangsan,[2] based on numerous field studies throughout the country, rejects the received idea that the drug traffic is the principal source of illicit money in Thailand, and it highlights the considerable dimensions of organized crime and local money laundering. To get a better idea of the systemic relations that have grown

133

up between the legal and illegal spheres, it may be useful to review the local political institutions.

The Thai political system was dominated, from 1945 until the mid-1980s, by rivalry between the military and civil bureaucracies, which share the revenues of corruption.[3] The culturally accepted dynamic of rent-seeking dominates all public markets and the acquisition of military materials. The political class has become wealthier, following the role model of Marshal Sarit, Prime Minister from 1957 to 1963, whose personal fortune was equivalent to 42 per cent of the State budget.[4] The civil and military bureaucracies are perceived as essentially *Thai* organizations, as opposed to the business circle which is dominated by Thai of Chinese origin, most of whom come from the Chaozhou district (Teochow), in the province of Guangdong. The 10 million Sino-Thai, constituting one-sixth of the population, dominate business, the big banks and the large private enterprises of the Bangkok region, under the paid protection of civil and military bureaucracies. In the north of the country, the 'irregular Chinese forces', remnants of the Kuomintang troops expelled after 1949, are allowed to function under an implicit agreement of protecting the country against communist expansion in exchange for having control of the illegal border trade in heroin and precious stones. In the 1970s, the 'Chinese irregular forces' were put directly under the control of Central Headquarters in Bangkok, which allowed them to stop all attempts to achieve autonomy by the minority mountain people, and to institutionalize the redistribution of narco-profits.

As of 1979, when domestic politics became more stable and elections were regular, 90 per cent of the parliamentary seats depended on the regions, allowing a new group of provincial economic elite, the *jao pho*, known as the *godfathers,* to expand their influence. The halting progress of democratization has resulted in political integration for the provinces, which contrasts with their economic backwardness: the provinces account for one-third of the country's enterprises, whereas the Bangkok area controls half of the national income and only fifteen per cent of the population. In the last two decades of the twentieth century, this contrast permitted the rise of the godfathers as an unassailable group in Thai politics. Most of the *jao pho* come from second- or third-generation Chinese immigrants originally from the Chaozhou district, in Guangdong, following the lead of 'other' Sino–Thai. Their new political role is closely related to their economic ascent, characterized by the interweaving of their legal and illegal activities. Originally offering counselling and providing agricultural loans to the population, which has remained largely rural despite the economic expansion, the *jao pho* diversified into trade, local monopolies such as the distribution of whisky, car and motorcycle sales, real estate and landowner speculation, construction and public works, illegal forest exploitation, smuggling, massage salons and prostitution, arms and drug trafficking.

The remarkable economic and political development of these new godfathers was documented in nine case studies conducted by Sungsidh Piriyarangsan and Pasuk Phongpaichit.[5] Many openly define themselves as 'half businessmen, half gangsters';[6] while others simply use their influence to develop their businesses and to pursue their political careers. They often employ a labour force of 'judiciary' gangsters, known as the *nak leng*, and organize friendly relations with the police and military hierarchies, who are then held under obligation to them. The Thai godfathers have in some way realized 'the quasi universal dream of all established entrepreneurs: the elimination of competition,'[7] but at the price of murderous conflicts which often cut short their existence. When their economic capital becomes consequent to the territory they control, they accumulate prestige through patronage and redistribution under the form of public investments useful to communities. The godfathers do not seek to conduct their affairs outside of the law but 'above the law',[8] seeing themselves as unassailable arbitrators who create peace 'on their pathway'. Hence, one of them boasts of being able to walk alone in his province of Petchburi, famous for its violence and blood crimes, without the presence of any body guard: 'I had enemies', he declares 'but they are all dead.'[9]

The direct or indirect quest for local and regional political power finally allows the *jao pho* to institutionalize their position. Their local networks of allegiances give them control of 'vote banks' indispensable to achieving an election victory. The illegal practice of the purchase of votes has in fact developed to epidemic proportions since 1949. The objective of the politicians is no longer to convince the electorate but to assure themselves of the loyalty of the new 'men of influence' who subcontract the vote promises to the chiefs of villages and to local civil servants. In the regions controlled by the godfathers, the coasts, the north and the northeast, where legal activities, smuggling and illegal revenues all flow together, elections in rural zones become a time of tension and of fear instead of an occasion for political debate. Violence is easily ignited with armed vote bank organizers often patrolling on behalf of rival candidates.[10]

Under the government of General Prem, 1980–88, the military and political bureaucracies took control of the new provincial elites by locking up the key ministers. But this alliance experienced problems with the leadership of the Chart Thai party, under the cabinets of General Chatichai (1988–91) and of Banharn (1995–96). Paraphrasing Clausewitz, the leaders of the Chart Thai define politics as the pursuit of business through different means. Banharn, who made a fortune in public works, expresses the opinion that 'for a politician, being in the opposition equals to starving yourself to death'.[11] The five-year leadership of the Chart Thai institutionalized the positions of the provincial godfathers, who had close ties with governors, regional commandants, and chiefs of police, and who monopolized the public works in their own areas. Following a series of scandals related to corruption, the Chatichai government was ousted in 1991 by a State military coup, the result of an alliance between the army and the civil and business circle bureaucracy of Bangkok. An investigation was conducted into 25 ministers; 13 were estimated as 'unusually rich', after having cashed numerous cheques from businessmen which related to public contracts.[12] But these results do not imply that any legal action can be taken, since the principal individuals have managed to redefine themselves in the unstable game of power coalitions.

This is the case, for example, for Narong Wongwan, known as the 'godfather of the North'. Having made an official fortune in tobacco, he became Minister of Agriculture under the Chatichai Government, and thereafter the most serious candidate for Prime Minister in 1992, under the military junta. His ambition was hindered by information that the USA suspected him of drug trafficking, to the extent of forbidding him to enter American territory.[13] This did not stop Narong Wongwan from trying to take the strategic position of Minister of the Interior during the government of Banharn, only to be arrested again for the same reasons. Other deputies were subject to the same accusations, such as Mongkol Chongsuttamanee, Thanong Siripreechapong – extradited to the USA in 1996 – and Vatana Asavahame, one of the leaders of Chart Thai.[14] In 1995–96, the Banharn Government was hit by a number of scandals implicating many ministers in real estate speculation and money laundering. Following threats to the press and the suppression of a television channel, the second coalition of the Chart Thai, which had led the way to central power for the provincial godfathers, suffered severe losses during the November 1996 elections, to the advantage of the cabinet headed by General Chavalit, who then ruled the 1997 crisis in a disastrous manner.

A former Chief of Staff who had returned to civilian life, Chavalit participated in the Chatichai Government (1988–91) and hoped to become Prime Minister. The creation of the New Action Party (NAP), after the 1991 State coup, favoured this objective. Chavalit initially relied on a network of the northeast godfathers to ensure himself of a loyal electorate, surrounded by the chiefs of villages and local officials. The day before the March elections in 1992, the General Secretary of the NAP, Prasong Soonsiri, resigned, criticizing 'the expansion policy of the NAP above all', which led him to accept 'men of influence' within his group, a euphemism designating the criminal godfathers.[15] The accusations were aimed in fact at Sia L., 'the godfather from the northeast', the son of Chinese immigrants in the 1930s, who made a fortune, besides the traditional *jao pho* monopolies, due to his control of an illegal lottery. A regular client of the big-time gamblers of Bangkok, who maintained very close relationships with the military and police hierarchy, Sia L. also depended on this protection to develop his business. 'I started poor and without education,' he declares, 'That's why I need to rely on friends and political relations for all that I undertake.'[16] Having survived many assassination attempts in Bangkok, where he intended to develop his activities, Sia L. received visits from the future chief of staff, from the capital's gambling tycoon, and even from the general secretary of the Democratic Party, a personal friend.

Having diversified his support for four political parties, during the 1988 elections, in 1992 Sia L. opted for the NAP of General Chavalit, for which he became the northeast regional co-ordinator. Among the 40 seats won by the NAP, 31 came from the northeast, which gave Chavalit's allied godfather considerable power over those he considered *his* deputies.[17] The rise of the NAP and the hostile positions it took over the military junta during the popular uprising of May 1992, which was put down by the army, allowed General Chavalit to occupy the post of Minister of the Interior in the coalition led by the Democratic Party of Chuan Leekpai, 1992–95. Despite the NAP's loss of credibility as the party of the masses, Chavalit used his position to consolidate his provincial political clientele, based on the buying of votes, even from deputies. In effect, this practice was developed during the July 1995 election, when certain well-established politicians accepted the equivalent of US$400 000–800 000 of 'transfer fees' to change political camps.[18]

The Democratic Party of Chuan Leekpai continued to be identified rather less with the politics of money, which was made easier by its dominance in the richer regions of

Bangkok and southern Thailand. But since it had not obtained an absolute majority, it was forced to form a coalition government with the new provincial elite in 1992–95, which precipitated its fall during a scandal related to agrarian reform. Its quest for power during the 1997 crisis did not remove the need for a governmental compromise with forces of the new assembly, this time more closely identified with the politics of money, for example the Social Action Party, which had 22 deputies, or with the dissidents of Prachakorn Thai, one of the smallest groups. The management of fragile and unstable coalition majorities gives a disproportionate influence to smaller parties. Many ministerial jobs were given to dissidents of Prachakorn Thai some of whom had been clearly identified as being involved in illegal gambling and drug trafficking. This was the case, for example, for Vatana Asvahame, known by the press as one of the 'godfathers of the North', who occupied the strategic position of Vice-Minister of the Interior. The USA has publicly suspected him of drug trafficking and laundering, and refused him an entry visa in 1995.[19]

The democratization of the Thai political system therefore appears to have been deeply influenced by territorial power struggles between regions which exhibited great inequalities, resulting in the institutionalization of illicit or criminal laundering activities. The vote buying, which represented one-quarter or one-third of the expenses of one candidate, increased the election expenses, which reached exorbitant dimensions: between US$800 000 and US$1 million for one northeastern candidate in 1995, and US$4 million in certain cases.[20] The 1995 electoral campaign cost US$680 million, the one in 1996, US$1–1.2 billion.[21] Apart from financing at the local level, often from godfathers, the principal political parties also receive private donations from banks and large corporations. The invisible force of metropolitan businessmen and central administration technocrats, sometimes allied with the Democratic Party, has weighed heavily on successive governments. In the eyes of the Bangkok elite, the rise of the provincial godfathers or of politicians related to them, comprises the principal threat against rational management of economic development.[22] The Thai political system is thus based on arbitrage and of redistribution between legal and illegal spheres, to such an extent that we may talk about the criminalization of institutions, along with the increasing influence of the illegal economy.

The police, for example, are seen as the most corrupt governmental service.[23] All officers who wish their career to progress rapidly must pay their superior. Financial donations to the police are not considered reprehensible, as long as they are voluntary. More than half of the police force are hired into 'protection' networks for jewellers, factories, massage salons, bars, warehouses and gambling establishments. The profits of these vast unionized rackets are redistributed within the police, where they feed the 'well-being funds', but are also distributed into the military hierarchy, the Ministry of the Interior and into the legal system. The racket has thus become a necessity of the job for the police, all the more so as they move up the promotion ladder. The particularly lucrative command posts are negotiated in effect within the black market: a general of the Thai police indicated that in 1990 a good provincial position would cost US$40 000. Command-level positions in Bangkok are at least ten times higher, and reached almost US$1 million in 1994, an amount equivalent to that required in Mexico for a lucrative command post along the border of the USA.[24] As illegal economy shareholders, one part of the Thai police force thus stimulates the development of super-profits, by encouraging the criminalization of society and of politics.

If this outline of the institutions gives an indication of the size of the illegal economy, its interaction with the formal economy largely depends on the dynamics of the legal economy, marked, as in Mexico, by the liberalization of trade and investments and the privatization of the public sector. From 1985 to 1991, Thailand was the principal beneficiary of the delocalization of the high labour-intensive activities of developed Asia (Japan, South Korea, Hong Kong, Taiwan, Singapore), which had been penalized by the consecutive monetary re-evaluations of the Plaza agreement of 1985, and by the rise of land and salary costs. The direct investment flows to textiles, clothing, toys, automobiles and electronics have allowed Thai exports to develop (from 28 to 41 per cent of GDP between 1985 and 1995). Bangkok's economic influence has grown with its neighbours, Burma, Cambodia, Laos and Vietnam, which had been trapped in underdevelopment. This keen interest of, mainly Asian, capital for Thailand led to a sharp re-evaluation of local assets: from 1987 to 1990 land values and securities increased by shocking proportions – between 10 or 20 times in certain cases.[25] Such an injection of money facilitates the rapid improvement of capital holders and favours the social rise of qualified workers and educated executives who form the new middle metropolitan class. Consumption increased tenfold in automobile sales in the cities, for example, in less than ten years (1985–95).

The privatization programme, launched in 1987–88, allows the capital available from the rise of real estate values and salaries to be tapped into by drawing investors towards the Stock market, more attractive to investors than the low interest rates on bank deposits. State enterprises are perceived as inefficient and corrupt (they served for a long time as rent-seeking sources for civil, military and political class bureaucracies) and the concession to the private sector of certain public infrastructures is supposed to put an end to the nightmare saturation of the transportation systems in the capital of Thailand. The Stock market, of very modest dimensions, becomes therefore an accumulation centre, where the traditional elite of the Prem years – including politicians, civil bureaucracies, the military, large Sino–Thai entrepreneurs – can build relationships with a new generation of provincial entrepreneurs, managers and financial men, often educated in foreign countries. In the absence of appropriate regulation, the rise of securities, in parallel with strong economic development, favours the speculative embezzlements of newcomers, guaranteed by politicians, who see in this market a source of finance that is cleaner and more sophisticated than the traditional corrupt funds, which are increasingly difficult to conceal.

The stock euphoria simultaneously generates an indebtedness among the middle classes, who borrow to buy lasting goods (real estate, automobiles, jewellery), or for the purchase of bonds, to the extent that private savings decreased from 20 to 8 per cent of their net revenues, from 1989 to 1995.[26] The creation of a Stock market control Commission in 1992 acted to curb some of the most worrisome embezzling, organized by the network of Sia Song, and involving investment funds worth US$800 million. As Paul Handley indicates, 'the term *Sia* is generally reserved for wealthy business men, most often of Chinese origin. It reflects the notion of both wealth and power and is frequently linked with "dark influences", in other words people who acquired their fortunes by semi-legal or illegal activities.'[27]

The closure of Sia Song's bond manipulation unions implicated 130 celebrities of the urban elite and of the political world, including General Chavalit, leader of the New Action Party, and two major actors of the Democratic Party. More surprising is the reaction that followed Sia Song. Instead of paying an honourable fine with regard to doubtful behind-the-scene investments and the embarrassing ramifications, Sia Song, accompanied by many deputies, threw himself into a regional crusade to denounce a real conspiracy among a number of prominent political and business leaders (for example, the Minister of Finance, Tarrin), against new entrepreneurs such as him, and representatives of the small shareholders of the middle classes. He charged that, in a spirit totally foreign to democracy, the bureaucratic elite had tried to monopolize the bond market, taking advantage of its access to valuable information with full impunity and preventing the new generation from taking profits.

Paul Handley legitimately underlines the pertinence of this defence: most of the bankers are important stock market investors as a result of their privileged access to confidential enterprise information. The leading women in politics and business also often intervene in the market. Therefore, no member of the financial community has escaped being cited or questioned following the scandal. It is very doubtful that Sia Song would have been able to manage funds of this size without the assistance of banks, financial houses and Stock market members. This impression seems to have been confirmed by the privatization policy of many large State enterprises, such as the Thai International airline company, PTT, the most important distributor of petroleum products, the ETA (Express way and Transit Authority of Thailand) and BECL (Bangkok Expressway Corporation Ltd). In all of these cases we witness the development of a grey market in undervalued bonds, reserved for managers, for civil and military bureaucrats, and for politicians. The accounting manipulations facilitate the rise of bonds and of profits collected by insider traders, without ameliorating the results of the enterprise and despite the fact that the State explicitly takes financial guarantees away from them.[28] The role of the Stock market in the allocation of financial resources thus appears to be perverted by the systematic practice of insider trading, which may involve the laundering of illegal funds.

This is not the case for foreign direct investments (FDI), 90 per cent of which are concentrated in the region of Bangkok, contributing to the increase of its economic and industrial weight compared to the rest of the country. With 70 per cent of FDI issued from developed Asia, the flows clearly slowed down around 1992, because of infrastructure congestion, the increase in property and labour costs, and the shortage of qualified personnel, related to delays in secondary and technical education. With the re-launch of its open policy and official adoption of the economic market in 1992, China became a fearsome competitor for all in Southeast Asia. Simultaneously, China took advantage of its geographic and cultural proximity to Hong Kong, Taiwan, Japan and South Korea, and of its labour costs being two to three times lower than those in Thailand. It also benefited from an abundance of qualified personnel, which quickly made it a privileged centre for the relocation of other Asian activities with high labour intensity and low added value. The dynamic of foreign investments in Thailand from this time was increasingly dictated by the penetration of a domestic market in full expansion, especially in the automobile sector which was dominated by Japanese companies. For the other sectors such as electronics or textiles, which respectively represented 23 per cent and 12 per cent of 1995 exports, the local added value remained weak, since 75–90 per cent of parts or raw materials were being imported.[29] The decrease of competitiveness in Thailand's economy was accentuated, after 1996, by the increasing value of the dollar which raised the prices of local exports, and by the reduction of the world demand for electronic and computer products, which affected all Asian countries. This was evident in the stagnation of exports in 1996, and the size of the current account deficit, which rose from 6 per cent to more than 8 per cent of GDP between 1993–94 and 1995–96.

Resorting to short-term foreign capital to finance the debt, a means employed since the 1980s, saw a considerable development during the 1990s, with the liberalization of currency control through credits, bond acquisitions on the Stock market, and mainly non-resident accounts. The differential of interest rates between foreign and Thai markets explains this tendency. In 1993, the creation of an offshore centre, the Bangkok International Banking Facility, reinforced the short-term capital flows, more than half of which transit through this facility. The direct foreign investments, introducing new technologies and ameliorating economic competition, decreased from 12 per cent to 1 per cent of the capital inflow to the private sector.[30] With direct foreign investments and exportation curbs, Thai growth has increasingly become dependent on theses short-term capital flows, accentuating the speculative drift of investments, largely directed towards the Stock market and real estate.

To feel reassured against the likelihood of a currency crisis and a depreciation of the baht, which would penalize their investments as happened in Mexico, international operators have insisted on the differences between the two countries. If the Thai foreign debt was higher than that of Mexico in 1994 (49 per cent of GDP as opposed to 35 per cent), it did not finance consumption, but consisted of a contribution to investment (43.8 per cent of GDP), supplementing an already high savings rate (34 per cent of GDP).[31] In reality, this analysis founders for two reasons. The first is that Thai savings essentially remained public. The authorities obtained budgetary surpluses both through orthodox financial policy and through negligence, that of fragmented administrations in unstable political conditions. They are also incapable of putting into place the massive infrastructure programmes that the country needs. Private savings have, as we have seen, decreased from 20 per cent to 8 per cent of net incomes between 1989 and 1995. This demonstrates that the short-term foreign debt financed the ostentatious consumption of the middle and upper classes, as in Mexico.

Secondly, the Thai investment rate (43.8 per cent of GDP) – high compared to Mexico (23.5 per cent in 1994) – does not reflect the efficiency of resource allocation, but the drifting of credits towards speculative real estate and over-capacity enterprise projects. The total credits given to the real estate sector at the end of 1996 were estimated at 800 billion baht dollars (US$31 billion), or 16 per cent of GDP, half of which (US$17 billion) consists of bad or un-payable loans. At the same time, there are as many as 350 000 unoccupied premises in Bangkok and 800 000 in the rest of the country. Two hundred golf courses have been constructed but only 20 per cent of the 400 000 Thai golfers have the means to join these clubs.[32] This speculative drifting of investment towards real estate, facilitated by the flow of short-term capital, evokes a parallel with Mexico. But the immoderate investment rate, which differs from Mexico's, cannot be simply explained by the importance of the public savings from the budgetary surplus accumulated since 1988, or by the short-term capital flow, which represented less than 10 per cent of GDP in the 1990s.[33] *This anomaly would be explicable only if the Thai financial system were recycling the considerable funds from the illegal economy with regard to the decrease of private savings and of limited auto-financing resources of enterprises.* To further explain this hypothesis, we must return to the specifics of this system.

The Thai monetary and financial circuits are dominated by the entrepreneurs of Chinese origin, in provinces such as Bangkok. Alongside the formal network of registered establishments, there coexists an informal system of loans and deposits with international connections. Thanks to the *huikuan*, literally the 'transfer of funds', created in the nineteenth century for the deposits of the emigrated Chinese from southeast Asia, it is possible to transfer sums of US$500 000 from Chieng Maï to Bangkok or from Bangkok to Hong Kong and New York, with a minimum of documents and a maximum of discretion, independent of legal banking procedures. A system of debt recognition and of mutual compensation, allows a locally deposited sum to be received from a non-official operator of another country. Jewellers, industrial societies, import–export companies or currency exchanges serve as channels for these parallel trades. They often belong to the same dialectical community of the Chaozhou Chinese, originally from Shantou, in the north of Guangdong province. These informal networks, quite similar to the *hawala* networks of south Asia, are used in a legal or illegal manner, for example by drug traffickers. The *huikuan* system has without doubt a negligible impact on Thai international payments, but this is not the case for the informal credit system, which may have a significant impact on the domestic economy by weakening formal credit.

The formal financial system was composed of commercial banks, financial societies and offshore banks. Ninety per cent of bank assets, evaluated at US$227 billion at the end of 1996, were controlled by domestic establishments, the first six of which managed 67 per cent of the total (Bangkok Bank, Krung Thaï, Thaï Farmers, Siam Commercial, Bank of Ayudhya, Thaï Military). The 91 financial societies, largely escaping from central bank supervision, represented, at the end of 1996, assets worth US$72 billion. Financed by loans or bills to which private individuals may subscribe, they are engaged in brokerage and credit operations, especially real estate. The offshore market (Bangkok International Banking Facility) relied on 46 banks, 15 of which were domestic, and the total of loans held was estimated, at the end of 1996, at US$51 billion, 60 per cent of which were currency loans for residents.[34]

The Bank of Thailand never practised a rigorous supervision of the financial system. The top level executives of the six principal banks may have been transferred from the Central Bank, or vice versa, which introduced a level of confusion between operators and supervisors. This confusion has been increased by the loss of Bank of Thailand's independence with regard to political power since the Banharn Government of 1995. Bear in mind that politicians are often stockholders of financial societies, that two of the six principal establishments, the Krung Thaï Bank and the Thaï Military Bank, are government and army properties, and that the Bangkok International Banking Facility escapes, by definition, from the supervision of the Central Bank, and the general picture is drawn of a financial system which is simultaneously speculative and dutiful to the political power. This enslavement constitutes, with the pursuit of growth which was dangerously initiated by the stagnation of exports in 1996, the perfect condition in which to pursue speculation; that is, a situation where national and international operators are convinced that the risk is totally safe, because if the private financial establishments are weak, these would be covered by the Bank of Thailand, since it is disposing of 8 years of budgetary excesses and of solid currency reserves.[35]

At the end of 1996, the burst of the real estate bubble followed the Stock market, launched at the beginning of the year. Of the US$90 billion of foreign debt, US$37 billion of which is short term, the equivalent of US$31 billion was loaned to promoters. Half of these funds passed through financial societies and represented unrecoverable debts.[36] The case of Finance One, the most important of all, is quite representative: in 1995, Finance One controlled almost 20 per cent of the Stock market transactions of Bangkok; its assets represented US$6 billion; real estate loans represented 30 per cent of the total portfolio and consumption credits 24 per cent. The young Chief Executive was surrounded by influential and famous people such as Vijit Supinit, governor of the Central Bank, and counted the Charoen Pokphand Group, the Paribas Bank and the Thai Farmers Bank among its stockholders.[37] At Finance One, as elsewhere, the fall of the stocks on the Stock market weakened company accounts, which plunged in the face of real estate overcapacity and non-payment by its debtors. But that was not the problem: the government formed a Fund for Financial Development Institutions, which bailed out private establishments in difficulty to a ceiling of US$19 billion, or 10 per cent of GDP, during the first quarter of 1997. The former Minister of Finance, Wiraphong Ramangkun, expressed his astonishment at the size of this aid, by underlining that the initial demand of the governor of the Bank of Thailand represented only a tenth of this amount. But this rescue operation by the political class would have only one limited use: instead of resolving the liquid asset problems of the establishments, most of the public funds that were given to them, with interest rates of 13 per cent, were just as quickly re-loaned to their clients at rates of 20 per cent, or were deposited in foreign countries.[38]

The rest of the Bank of Thailand reserves ran out in a fierce parity defence of the currency against the dollar, especially on the futures market, by promising to buy bahts, in the following three, six, nine or twelve months, at US$23.4 billion. Following this imprudent defence, the real currency reserves were only US$800 million in May 1997, while the

Bank officially displayed reserves of US$38 billion.[39] The disparity between these two figures reveals the size of the currency crisis, which began with the decision to let the baht float at the beginning of July, facilitated by the urgent aid plan of the IMF to the tune of US$17 billion. The closure of 56 out of 91 insolvent financial companies, a requirement of the international fund creditors, was undertaken only after a long period of negotiations, during which the Chavalit government tried to recapitalize public funds, before its fall in November 1997 under public pressure. The currency crisis was thus transformed into a financial, economic and political crisis, highlighting the considerable responsibilities of the leadership.

One year later, its total cost was estimated at US$128 billion, or 100 per cent of the GDP of 1998, if we take into account the fall of 50 per cent of the stock index and more than 70 per cent of the currency rate with regard to the dollar. This has also brought up the reimbursement rate of local creditors. Of the 35 financial societies remaining after December 1997, there are now only 28 in existence and the recapitalization cost of the banking system has been estimated at more than US$20 billion, more than the entire current capitalization of the Stock market.[40]

Unemployment has risen and the recession reduced the GDP by at least 4 per cent in 1998. The fact that the crisis spread across the southeast Asia region explains its depth, with disengagements of other southeast Asian currencies against the dollar, and the repercussions of the Thai weakness on the Japanese banks, which financed half of the short-term debt of the country (not to mention investments and Korean debts in southeast Asia, which climbed to US$15.5 billion).[41] The relaunch of Thai exports, half of which are directed towards Asia, is constrained by the regional perspectives of the recession. It must be noted that, over and above this international aspect, the structural roots of the crisis remain alive.

The entire financial system institutionalized laundering, in the Stock market, in financial societies and in regional branches of national banks, who live under the influence of local godfathers.[42] This institutionalization is the logical consequence of the absence of a law against laundering, except for the particular case of drug trafficking, which apparently concerns limited amounts. Banking confidentiality is ferociously respected and the Thai authorities have always been opposed to the extension of the notion of laundering in illegal activities, which finances increasingly costly election campaigns. When politics is conceived as 'the pursuit of business by other means', the result is constant efforts to bring returns on investments, whether by embezzlement in infrastructure projects and the public equipment market (for an average of 30–40 per cent of such budgets),[43] or by bond manipulation and speculative investments. The recycling of illegal funds produces, in effect, artificial growth effects on the economy, by feeding the real estate bubble, the Stock market and consumption. The flow of short-term foreign capital reinforces this dynamic, by increasingly weakening local competivity, up to the point of open crisis, which leads to the socialization of losses.

The responsibility of the government is so evident that one of the priorities for Thailand, in the management of the crisis, is to have a new constitution to limit the role of money in politics.[44] While it is yet too soon to pronounce the success or failure of institutional reform, certain signs illustrate the continuity of the system. Sungsidh wrote:

'In the preceding Assembly, twenty to thirty parliamentarians held illegal activities which allowed them to buy their votes for re-elections. The profits of illegal activities are easy, important and not taxable. Their recycling in regular affairs places honest entrepreneurs on the bench and creates an artificial inflation in real estate, where the prices do not decrease despite the crisis.'[45]

The ascendancy of laundering thus slows down the stabilization process of the financial system, despite the nationalization of certain banks or the recapitalization of the six largest establishments, used to deposit funds for their bad debts. The most rigorous criteria on the framing of credit, introduced by the Bank of Thailand anxious to align the local practices with international practices, brought about an increase in interest rates on loans, which sometimes reached more than 16 per cent. The operators then have a tendency to move back into the informal credit networks. By accentuating the recycling of illegal funds and the unequal competition that they introduce, these networks enjoy a revival.[46] In these conditions, the stabilization of the financial system may slow down the speed to the advantage of the illegal economy, thus distorting the allocation of resources towards less competitive sectors, and accentuating debt and the dependence on foreign countries.

Notes

1 Cf. *Nord–Sud Export Conseil*, 22 February 1997. The importance of the sex industry is confirmed in a recent report of the ILO (International Labor Organization), which estimates that it accounts for up to 14 per cent of the GDP in Indonesia, Malaysia, the Philippines and Thailand (cf. *Le Monde*, 22 August 1998).

2 Cf. The Thai Journal *Phuchatkan*, Bangkok, 6 October 1997 in SWB BBC Asia-Pacific, 9 October 1997; Michael Vatikiotis and Bertil Lintner, *Far Eastern Economic Review*, 11 May 1995 and 8 May 1997; *La Dépêche internationale des drogues*, no. 75, January 1998. Thailand has at least 214 000 heroin addicts, according to official statistics.

3 Cf. Sungsidh Piriyarangsan and Pasuk Phongpaichit, *Democracy and Corruption in Thailand*, Chieng Maï, Silkworm Books, 1996.

4 Ibid., p. 52.

5 Ibid., ch. 3.

6 Ibid., p. 69.

7 Cf. Diego Gambetta and Peter Reuter, 'The mafia in legitimate industries', in Gianluca Fiorentini and Sam Peltzman, *The Economics of Organized Crime*, Cambridge University Press, 1997, p. 133.

8 Sungsidh Piriyarangsan and Pasuk Phongpaichit, *Democracy and Corruption*, p. 61.

9 Ibid., p. 78.

10 Cf. Surin Maisrikrod and Duncan MacCargo, 'Electoral Politics', in Kevin Hewison (ed), *Political Change in Thailand, Democracy and Participation*, London, Routledge, 1997, pp. 135 and 136.
11 Cf. Pasuk Phongpaichit and Chris Baker, 'Power in transition: Thailand in the 1990s', in Hewison, *Political Change*, p. 31.
12 Cf. Sungsidh Piriyarangsan and Pasuk Phongpaichit, *Democracy and Corruption*, p. 14.
13 Ibid., p. 81.
14 Cf. Thitinan Pongsudhirak, 'Thailand's media, whose watchdog?', in Hewison, *Political Change*, p. 226.
15 Cf. Duncan MacCargo, 'Thailand's political parties', in Hewison, *Political Change*, pp. 128–29.
16 Cf. Sungsidh Piriyarangsan and Pasuk Phongpaichit, *Democracy and Corruption*, p. 75.
17 Ibid., pp. 75–6.
18 Maisrikrod and MacCargo, 'Electoral politics', pp. 137–8.
19 Cf. *Far Eastern Economic Review*, 16 April 1998. The Social Action Party, a member of the Democratic coalition headed by Chuan Leekpaï, is perceived as the most corrupt political force after the Thai Chart. It is led by Montri Pongpanich, one of the police officers accused of unexplained wealth after the Military State coup of 1991 (Cf. Sungsidh Piriyarangsan and Pasuk Phongpaichit, *Democracy and Corruption*, pp. 156–7). Cf. also Suchitra Punyaratabandhu, 'Thailand in 1997: Financial crisis and constitutional reform', *Asian Survey* no. 2, February 1998; *La Dépêche internationale des drogues*, DGO, Paris, no. 79, May 1998.
20 Maisrikrod and MacCargo, 'Electoral politics', p. 139.
21 Hewison, *Political Change*, p. 2.
22 Pasuk Phongpaichit and Baker, 'Power in transition', p. 29.
23 Sungsidh Piriyarangsan and Pasuk Phongpaichit, *Democracy and Corruption*, ch. 4, 'Corruption in the police' and following chapters.
24 Cf. Peter Andreas, 'The political economy of narco-corruption in Mexico', *Current History*, April 1998.
25 The following information largely connects with the study of Paul Handley, 'More of the same: Politics and business, 1987–1996', in Hewison, *Political Change*' pp. 95–113.
26 Ibid., p. 102.
27 Ibid., p. 268.
28 Ibid, pp. 109–13.
29 Cf. *The Far East and Australia*, 1998, p. 1075.
30 Cf. Toshio Tanaka (1996) 'Baht economy and financial deregulation', quoted in *China Newsletter JETRO*, no. 133, 1998, vol. 2, pp. 11, 14, 15.

31 Cf. *Financial Times*, 9 August 1996.

32 Cf. *Far Eastern Economic Review*, 21 August 1997 and *Nord–Sud Export Consultants*, 22 February 1997 and 27 April 1997.

33 The pre-eminence of the public savings over the private savings is one of the specifics of the Thai economy compared to the Asian capitalist economies. Between 1980 and 1985, for example, the public savings represented 14.3 per cent of GDP and the private savings 4.7 per cent, or 19 per cent of the savings rate, quite low among southeast Asia countries. In the 1990s, the budgetary surplus represented each year, up until the crisis, about 3 per cent of GDP.

34 Cf. F. Lakhoua, 'La crise financière thaïlandaise', *Epargne sans frontières* no. 46, March–April 1997.

35 Cf. *Financial Times*, 12 January 1998, p. 6.

36 Lakhoua, *'La crise'*.

37 Cf. Emmanuelle Boulestreau, *Chronique d'une catastrophe annoncée: Corée, Thaïlande, Indonésie* ..., Paris 1998, pp. 115–17.

38 Cf. *Thaï Rat*, Bangkok, 12 August 1997, in SWB BBC Asia-Pacific, 15 August 1997; *Far Eastern Economic Review*, 4 September 1997.

39 Cf. Declaration of the economic counsellor of the Prime Minister Chuan Leekpai, *Thaï Rat*, Bangkok, 15 April 1998, in SWB BBC Asia-Pacific, 22 April 1998.

40 Cf. Declaration of the State Secretary of Finance, Pisit Leeahtam, *Financial Times*, 19 May 1998; *The Economist*, 8 August 1998, p. 66.

41 Cf. Federation of Korean Industries, Yonhap news agency, Seoul, 17 February 1998, in SWB BBC Asia-Pacific, 18 February 1998. 60 per cent of the invested or loaned funds by the Koreans, or US$9.3 billion, are directed to Indonesia and Thailand.

42 Cf. Michael Vatikiotis, *Far Eastern Economic Review*, 16 April 1998.

43 Cf. Sungsidh Piriyarangsan and Pasuk Phongpaichit, *Democracy and Corruption*, p. 164.

44 Cf. Suchitra Punyaratabandhu, quoted article, p. 165.

45 Cf. Emmanuelle Boulestreau, p. 141.

46 Cf. Michael Vatikiotis, *Far Eastern Economic Review*, 16 April 1998.

Conclusion

It may be useful to elaborate on some of the points which have emerged in this voyage through time and space. The first concerns the inseparable relationship between drug trafficking and transnational organized crime. The observation of localised situations has demonstrated that the networks are not solely organized around drugs. Sometimes mass criminal activity is involved, such as in the case of Mexico, which takes advantage of its proximity to the great American market; but the economic influence of drug trafficking seems to be more limited in certain transit countries, such as China and Thailand, or in metamphetamine consumer countries such as Japan.

However, if one acknowledges that narco-trafficking profits are an integral part of the very diversified grey and black economies, the question takes on a different magnitude. In Japan, as in Mexico and Thailand, the criminal economy develops, on the base of systematic corruption, a tradition of tolerance towards organized crime and more expensive political systems. Hence, it has become difficult to distinguish the criminal economy from the legal economy and from the power of certain political parties. The laundering dynamic creates the right conditions for a progressive institutionalization of the criminal world, but in doing so it unbalances the financial system which constitutes its centre of gravity. By twisting competition to its profit, laundering takes advantage of speculation, at the expense of production. It emphasizes the development of real estate and stock bubbles until it forces a crisis situation. This transfers the bad debts to the community, a significant proportion of which have originated in the illegal and criminal economy.

The socialization of losses coexists with the privatization of Mafia profits. In the Japanese case, the *yakuza* weakens the economy, by threatening the liquidation of the banks' real estate liabilities, and sometimes by profiting from the complicity of the indebted banks or of certain financial companies. In the case of Mexico, the laundering dynamic has been supplied by continuous flows of money and thus increased the illegal economy's power over the financial system. Competition has been reduced, to the advantage of those banks active in recycling narco-dollars. In the case of Thailand, where drug trafficking is only a minor part of the illegal economy, the crisis leads to a backward surge of the formal financial sector to the advantage of the informal sector, by reinforcing the laundering influence.

In all three cases, the responsibilities of certain political circles appear to have been a determining factor, since exorbitant election expenses have been partially financed by the recycling of these same illegal funds. We have, in fact, the right to question whether this inflation of election costs, generally proportionate to the practice of buying votes and of high abstention rates, reflects the internationalization of an American-style marketing policy or Mafia-style investment strategies in the political realm, counting on clientele support. The works of Christian Geffray on the consequences of drug trafficking in the Brazilian Amazon,[1] or the political development in Mexico and in Thailand, not to mention Columbia, show that these two tendencies may coexist. Exactly like criminal investment in the political sphere may contribute to the inflation of election expenses, and distort competition to the detriment of candidates who have only limited resources.

The relationships between organized crime, laundering and financial crises are not necessarily automatic. This can be observed in the extension of Thailand's crisis through cascading depreciation into Korea, a victim of industrial overcapacity financed by short-term capital, and in China, whose development rests to a large extent on direct Japanese and NIE investments, concentrated in highly labour-intensive export activities. All of these countries suffer from systemic corruption which has diverted the allocation of resources and undermined confidence in financial intermediation. The contagion effects rely upon the regionalization of investment and trade, half of which are internal to the zone. Japan and Thailand, which played crucial roles in the crisis – in the first case as master of the art of Asian regionalization and in the second as a catalyst – have both experienced a qualitative jump from the systemic corruption stage to that of the progressive criminalization of the financial sphere. From this point of view, the Asian crisis is not reducible to one cyclic problem of painful adjustment, but it poses a structural and institutional problem, referring to the democratization of political regimes and to their capacity to install a legal system, independent of authoritative powers. The diversity of the development levels and of local political cultures, the resilient factors that we have seen at work, are poor predictors of this longer and more complex transition, reminding us of the occurrences during the debt crisis and the lost decade of the 1980s in Latin America.

On the other hand, other Asian countries passed from systemic corruption to progressive economic and political criminalization, preventing any relationship between crisis and laundering. This has been the case in Cambodia, the true paradise of criminal profit recycling for the Chinese from Bangkok, Hong Kong, Taiwan and the Japanese *yakuza*. It is on the way to becoming a narco-State.[2] It is also the case in the Philippines where, according to senator Ernesto Herrera, a specialist on drug issues, drug traffickers generate an annual turnover of US$ 9 billion for the Chinese Mafia, or 10 per

cent of the 1996 GDP, by developing corruption within the
police, customs, army, justice and governmental and political
realms.[3] Finally, in Taiwan, organized crime and the security
of the citizens have become the second national preoccupa-
tion following the management of relations with Continental
China. The crime rate increased by 80 per cent in the first half
of the 1990s.[4] Following a number of assassinations, including
eight members of the district council of Taoyuan (1996), the
feminist and opposition member, Peng Wan-ju, who was
raped then executed, and the only daughter of a television
star, Justice Minister Liao Cheng-hao evoked the possibility
of a Sicilian island drift: according to official statistics, 35 per
cent of the members of municipal and district councils elected
in 1994, and 10 per cent of the deputies, had an association
with organized crime.[5] Gangs, who until that time were
confined to prostitution, gambling and drug trafficking, have
developed due to construction and the temptations of public
markets at the local level.[6] Today, they finance and manage
the purchasing of votes and the election expenses of certain
candidates, giving rise to costs of an average of US$1–1.5
million for a seat in the legislative assembly.[7] 'Mafia
capitalism', related to the economic development of organized crime, is often denounced as a threat to the
democratization of Taiwanese society.[8] But although the
Justice Minister may point out the involvement of gangsters
in certain stock embezzlements,[9] the Mafia penetration into
the financial system has not, for the moment, given way to
significant imbalances. In the cases of Cambodia and Taiwan,
the recession or the deceleration of economic activity is
essentially due to exogenous factors related to the regionalization of the crisis. The political dynamics of these three
countries illustrate, however, a worrying tendency that we
have seen demonstrated in Thailand, and which may make its
appearance in China at any time: the democratization process
of regimes is increasingly used as a Trojan horse by organized
crime elements. The economic rise of those operating
'outside the law' is allowing these people to move from the

margins of economic activity to become people with social and political positions which may put them 'above the law' by financing political parties or directly profiting from parliamentary immunity. Nevertheless, this tendency is not confined to Asia: the dangerous liaisons between the democratization of regimes and the rise of organized crime can be equally well observed in post-communist countries such as Russia.

The second piece of evidence that deserves to be highlighted concerns the consolidation of world inequality[10] and of elite powers through narco-trafficking. There is an added value level estimated at 85–90 per cent for heroin and cocaine in the large northern hemisphere consumer countries.[11] Europe and the USA are hence the great profit makers; the price of drugs can be multiplied by a factor of 40–100 as it crosses transit zones.[12] Inequality increases once again with the laundering of narco-profits via offshore centres and the international financial system.

At the other extreme, the producer countries take a derisory proportion of the added value in absolute terms: US$1.2 billion, at the most, for Burma, US$2–5 billion for Columbia. In relative terms, the locally laundered funds have an impact that is just as important when countries are poor. The surplus of narco-currency has a tendency to revalue the local currency, penalizing the competition of legal exports and encouraging the import of consumer goods from industrial countries, representing 40 per cent of total purchases in the case of Burma. This tendency is accentuated by the concentration of investment in the property and real estate sectors, generally a net importer. The country then falls into what economists call the Dutch disease, referring to the strong dependency that the Netherlands has experienced on exports of its natural gas. Diversification of the economy is blocked, development comes to rely increasingly on drugs, and the balance of payments suffers.[13]

To these economic problems we must add the human and social cost of the conflicts. Production zones are torn up, societies are divided and local political regimes are damaged in the Golden Triangle, the Golden Crescent and the Andean countries. The considerable extension of the drug consumption in producer and transit countries constitute a new problem in the 1990s, to such an extent that the division between production, trafficking, consumption and laundering zones is diminishing, as is the case in Mexico and Thailand. For example, it is estimated that almost half of the world's supply of heroin is available in the large European and American markets. The rest is consumed in production and transit countries, seized by the authorities or lost during the transportation.[14]

The increase of economic dependence and the health, social and institutional problems related to drugs may also, once again, increase in a new form of geopolitical dependence. What comes to mind here is the 'war on drugs' launched by the USA in Latin America, becoming in the post-Cold War period the principal mission of US Army forces in the southern hemisphere. When local police forces are acknowledged to be corrupt, the task of repression is assigned to the military. This may compromise the process of democratization under way at the same time that corrupt investments are now aimed at the armed forces, who prove no more transparent than the police. Perpetuating the dependence of the sub-continent, the potential consequences of this policy were underlined with an incisive irony by the former Bolivian President, Gonzalez Sanchez de Lozado: 'when you have a corrupt chief of police you fire him; but when you have a corrupt chief of the Army, it is he that fires you.'[15]

As a former Assistant Secretary of State for International Narcotics Matters has affirmed, the new American narco-diplomacy, with its annual 'certification' procedures, publishes bulletins of good conduct attributed to countries who are positively engaged in the drugs struggle, highlighting the idea that drug problems essentially come from foreign countries. Almost 70 per cent of the federal budget is centred around the suppression of trafficking, at the expense of more efficient prevention and care programmes. This, however, has not stopped the sharp increase in American production of marijuana, LSD, amphetamines and ecstasy, and the 50 per cent decrease in the retail price of heroin and cocaine since the beginning of the 1980s.[16] Since the problem is not merely one of arbitrating between strategies focused on supply or demand, the failure of the 'war on drugs' should lead to fundamental rethinking.

If you consider that 'the enemy in the drug war is not an army or a foreign insurrection, but an economic market,'[17] the centre of gravity, or in Clausewitzian terms, the pivot of power, or 'the point against which all of the energies must be directed', is not the demand for drugs (which may be reduced by a policy of prevention and care) but the considerable financial profits made at the trafficking and especially at the laundering stage, the only criminal activity allowing profits to be maximized by minimizing risks.

The contrast between the effective criminalization of drug consumption and the quasi impunity that the laundering of narco-profits enjoys is not due to the lightness of legal dispositions. The Financial Action Task Force (FATF), nominated after the Arche summit in 1989, created or reinforced anti-laundering legislation for its numerous country members. The Vienna Convention in 1988, signed within the framework of the United Nations, gives countries who wish to have legal recourse, an opportunity to reverse the onus of proof in order to determine the origin of illegal profits. This essential strategic clause forces trafficking or laundering suspects to prove the legal origin of their goods. The accusations are, however, very often blocked when they are obliged to show the illegal origin. Countries of the Council of Europe extended this disposition in 1990 to criminal activities, but it is national legislatures or regulatory practices that must take the necessary step. The Geneva Appeal, launched in 1996 and signed by 500 European magistrates, denounced the obstacles to legal co-operation within the Union, by asking for an effective application of the

Schengen accords, which ensure 'the transmission of inter-national rogatory commission and of the investigation results between judges, without interference of the executive power and without resort to the diplomatic path.'[18]

The gap between the judiciary and police protectionism and the transnational power of organized crime is attributed to the absence or the hesitancy of political will. This sometimes refers to the anxieties caused by investigations of fund embezzlement or the illegal financing of various parties. In this spirit, the 'power of judges' is often invoked in Europe as a threat that affects the political stability, instead of being envisaged from the point of view of responsibilities, which are to be fulfilled by authorities of the executive power. But in addition to these hindrances, the absence or hesitancy of the political will can also be due to economic reasons.

The logic and objectives of the financial deregulation and globalization of trades will dominate the international agenda of the next decade. The only rule that financial globalization acknowledges is that of self-regulation by the market; it is external to political will and is concretely situated in an *out of law* space. In the global context, the IMF and the World Bank have insisted on the beneficial effects of the new dynamic. New markets have opened for the northern countries, leading to growth, foreign capital and job creation among their southern partners. As a result, drug trafficking and, more generally, the economic expansion of grey zones and organized crime are considered as partial and negative consequences of a positive global movement. Their economic effects, mainly analysed through the example of Andean countries, are those most often reduced to the 'Dutch disease' aggravating the dependence of producer countries, without which the transit or laundering role in the great industrialized countries is inexplicable. At a more diffused level, the idea exists that laundering allows illegal capital to be functionally integrated, by operating Keynesian type increased effects.

This view is evidently simplistic for various reasons. First, the dynamic of the globalization of trade, the structural adjustment policies in the Third World and the difficulties of post-communist transitions create strong socio-spatial disparities, while increasing exclusion, unemployment and attempts to escape from these forces, through illegal activities.[19]

Second, the functionalist analyses of corruption tend to neglect its devastating political consequences. The idea 'that it is better to corrupt a police officer than to attack the police station'[20] implies that corruption has a positive effect in easing social relations, which would favour the emergence of new elites, who are supposed to be functional or modern compared to the old ones (in the image of the bourgeois class relative to the aristocracy of the Ancien Regime). This is not the case for criminal elites who prosper in the framework of the post-communist transition or in the case of new autocracies or democracies in Africa.[21] The criminalization of a series of States poses new political and geopolitical problems, the consequences of which are unpredictable.

Lastly, by looking at three major financial crises of the post-Cold War period, in Japan, Mexico and Thailand, we have considered the so-called functionality of the recycling of drug and organized crime profits. Despite the considerable differences between these countries in terms of their economic sizes, cultures and political systems, laundering of organized crime has accelerated, in all of the cases, real estate and stock speculation; it has insensibly modified the rules of the game by means of threat and violence, distorted competition to its advantage, and concluded with a crisis on a national and international collectivization of loss and debts which are partly of Mafia origin.

This is also demonstrated by the Russian financial crisis, which offers another example of the relationship between destabilization and laundering of the illegal economy. According to the high estimates made by Interpol, organized crime may control today 40 per cent of the GDP. The Russian economy abandoned production in favour of speculation: the bank loans in the real sector represent only 10 per cent of GDP, while the ratio is often more than 100 per cent in Western countries.[22] The accumulation of the budgetary deficit is directly at the heart of the confidence crisis of local financial operators and the withdrawal of foreign investment portfolios, which had become the most productive in the world. According to Venyamin Sokolov, director of the Russian Federation Chamber of Accounts, 'fiscal revenues are solely collected in order to be stolen. The losses at the federal and regional level are considerable.' On the US$3 billion invested, for example, for the reconstruction of Chechnya, only US$150 million has been transferred. No one is able to say what has happened to the rest. The massive privatization programme launched by Boris Yeltsin should have bailed out the federal budget, but it was quickly transformed into a clearance sale of public assets without ameliorating the results of the great majority of the enterprises concerned. The domestic debt service today absorbs 45 per cent of State receipts paralysing the entire support to national education, public health and scientific research.[23] The most astonishing fact in these conditions is that since 1996 Switzerland has become (according to the estimates) the first or second largest investor in Russia, by openly recycling exported Russian capital from the depletion of public assets, extortion and organized crime.[24]

Thus, there is a sort of attraction of capital looking for the highest returns, highest productivity, from Mexico, to Thailand then to Russia, and the criminalization of economies, which increase the particularly profitable speculative tendencies of financial capital. The example of Russian–Swiss investments in Russia also shows that a proportion of the foreign direct investment and of short-term capital may originate in illegal or criminal activity. If this is the case, we would witness a progressive convergence between the poles of local laundering and the poles of international laundering, under a general framework of strong speculative pushes and repeated financial crises.

This hypothesis is quite serious. If one adds the annual laundering of drug money, worth US$100 billion, the same amount for organized crime activities, and all offshore capital from the grey illegal economy (fiscal evasion, international commissions, public asset embezzlement, etc.) which cannot be less than the first two, the annual total of laundering would have to be estimated at US$400 billion. In an IMF document, Vito Tanzi even quoted an amount of US$500 billion.[25] If these statistics were correct, annual laundering would represent 6–7 per cent of the net international financial needs, estimated at US$6400 billion in 1995. But despite its limited dimension, laundering may affect the conduct of the strongest operators of the market like the institutional investors of the rich countries (pension and mutual funds), which manage US$26 000 billion, half of which belongs to the USA. The very attractive returns on capital in most financial centres market by laundering, in fact, pushes them to diversify their portfolio to the profit of their destinations, by accentuating the monetary destabilization of the emergent countries. *The attraction between the criminalized economies and the international capital flows thus reproduces that between laundering and speculative sectors at the local level.*

At certain points, laundering effects reflect the mirror of history. The situation that has existed since 1830 with the massive extension of opium commerce between the British Indies and China created a form of *out of law* colonial law in the Middle Empire. Drug supplies have thus experienced an exponential development. Combined with the competition between traffickers, it contributes to the decrease of prices and to the development of consumption, similar to the post-Cold War situation. Economic criminality managed to make itself, during the Opium Wars, and with the help of a corrupt power, an integral part of, and even indispensable to, the real economy; this assures the financing of the local State and contributes to the dysfunctional reproduction of the system. The development of organized crime in the financial world seems to recreate this movement; the criminal economy thus becomes an integral part and agent of the real economy. The illegal sphere is always situated *under the condition of the legal sphere. But it slowly submits this latter to a purely speculative logic*, through its research of high financial productivity.

As in the nineteenth century, there are conflicts in the sharing of criminal added value: the endogenous part of the drug supply, which has intervened in China since 1880, is similar to the development of local production of LSD, ecstasy and marijuana in the USA in the 1980–1990s. The dynamic of money laundering from the illegal economy, from drugs and organized crime, seems to produce similar conflicts: essentially concentrated in the large western countries and their offshore dependencies until the beginning of the 1990s, it has had a tendency to be diffused thereafter towards the south and post-communist countries with the deregulation of trade and the reinforcement of legal frameworks in northern countries. But contrary to the situation in the nineteenth century, where the geo-economy and the geopolitics of drugs created conflicting relations or economic effects of a bilateral form, such as between England and China, the integration of financial markets has reinforced the destabilizing effects of laundering at the international level.

The case of China, situated at the problematic centre of post-communist countries and developing countries, also illustrates this general tendency. The attraction that has emerged between Switzerland and Russia, orchestrating the massive recycling of illegal and criminal profits, is naturally reproduced between the Chinese continent and Hong Kong's offshore banking facilities. The laundering of criminal money, without doubt, plays a significant role, particularly if we include the 'annex' of Hong Kong, Macao. Its impact, however, remains relatively negligible in terms of the illegal economy. We have seen, for example, that drug trafficking generates a turnover of US$3.6 billion, according to official Chinese statistics.[26] If we make the assumption that the annual heroin consumption, 40 tons, is underestimated by half, domestic trafficking would then represent a maximum of

US$7 billion, an amount comparable to US$6 billion estimated on the drug market in Russia or Japan.[27] These amounts do not include the international Burmese heroin trafficking, frequently financed by Hong Kong, nor the recycling of profits, carried out in the former British colony and in Macao.[28] They also do not take into account the considerable profits from prostitution – developed on an industrial scale in the province of Guangdong – from clandestine gambling, smuggling and labour force trafficking, which in most cases comes from Hong Kong and the Taiwan Triads. The International Migration Organization, based in Geneva, estimated, for example, that between 1989 and 1996, almost 1 million Chinese economic refugees entered the USA or Europe by illegal immigration channels, costing between US$26 000 and US$40 000 per trip.

Whatever the profits of organized crime in China – something which has not yet been studied – its laundering certainly does not reach Thai dimensions, relative to a gross domestic product of more than US$900 billion in 1997. On the other hand, the economic reforms and the opening policy, which are reflected by a conversion of bureaucratic power, into the power to appropriate public assets, and generate rent-seeking, according to economist Wang Anpei, estimated at 32 per cent of the national income in 1992.[29] In the absence of a legal framework, laundering has been focused on the property, real estate and stock market speculation. It has generated a grey securities market which provoked, in 1992, riots of small holders conned at the Stock market of Shenzhen, near Hong Kong, and developed a real estate overcapacity of 300 million square metres in 1997, that is more than three million homes and empty offices, the equivalent of urban construction for one year.[30]

Between 1992 and 1994, at the time of the renewal of the opening policy, Chinese cities became the scene of a vast embezzlement of public land, to the advantage of local authorities and in close collaboration with large Hong Kong groups, who had at least half of their investments in China centred on property and real estate. If we focus on the example of Hong Kong, where the Public Treasury at the time received US$3.6 billion per square kilometre sold to property developers, the city of Peking would have gained US$18 billion, since prices were on average three times lower in the Chinese capital. The municipality, in fact, only received US$300 million for all of the transactions.[31] The mayor of Peking, also a member of the political bureau of the CCP, Chen Xitong, was finally arrested on charges of corruption. The accusations blame him for US$2 billion missing from municipality chests; however the amount is without doubt ten times higher, and represents for him alone 2 per cent of Chinese GDP.

This simple example illustrates the extension of domestic laundering related to the embezzlement of public funds, which also concerns the financial sector. We therefore estimate that not less than 30 per cent of the improved credits destined for the State sector are re-loaned by public enterprises to non-state sectors, ready to pay interest rates that are twice as high.[32] If the grey and black financial markets are only infrequently analysed in China,[33] privatization policies also give birth to very fragile stock markets. More than 740 companies are listed on the Stock market for a total capitalization of US$5500 billion. But according to economists Xiao Zuoji, Liu Hongru and Wu Jinglian, numerous local governments rated the poorer performing enterprises, with the sole objective of recapitalizing them thereafter.[34]

If we now analyse the foreign laundering extensions, the interactions made with the Hong Kong financial centre are striking. The depletion of public assets in China is officially estimated at US$8 billion per year since 1985.[35] This amount must be considered in the context of capital flights from the continent, estimated at US$6.5–8.5 billion per year during the same period, by the Chinese government, and at US$10 billion according to Hong Kong bankers in the 1990s.[36] If we consider these estimates, capital flights from China would be at least equivalent to one-third of foreign direct investment, estimated at US$200 billion at the end of 1997. Hence we generally estimate that 20–30 per cent of the direct foreign investment from Hong Kong to China, in other words US$24–35 billion, is fed by the recycling of capital flights from the continent for fiscal or customs 'optimization' reasons. The Russian–Swiss scheme is thus well established in the Chinese case, but it feeds a powerful destabilization operation on both sides of the border, on the basis of real estate and stock speculation.

At the continent level, bad debts are officially valued at 25 per cent of bank loans, in other words 20 per cent of GDP.[37] These difficulties may not be reduced to the State enterprise deficit, unless we integrate, into their accounts, the massive embezzlement of public credit, principally carried out to the advantage of the real estate speculation. With regard to Hong Kong, Chinese capital flights have fed, over two years, strong real estate speculation by increasing the prices by 50 per cent – while this sector represents one-quarter of GDP and 40 per cent of local stock capitalization.[38] It is in this local context, that one must consider the expansion of the Asian crisis in China and Hong Kong, without neglecting the competitive pressure of the currencies' depreciations which has hit the entire zone, the fall of foreign investments as well as the reduction of the market of developed Asia.

We have definitely found all of the elements which contribute to the progressive criminalization of the economy on a world level: the inter-penetration between the black economy, still at a local level, and the grey economy, already considerable; the core of offshore banking, generating speculative tendencies; and the attraction that it creates in international financial trades, that know no other law than that of self-regulation by the market and its periodic crisis. Today the emerging countries are the most threatened, to the extent that deregulation policies, the liberalization of capital flows and the privatization of public monopolies offer, as we have seen in Mexico and in Thailand, ideal conditions for the laundering of dirty money, in a general context of devalorization of the legal framework. In this sense, the laundering virus today contaminates the vast programme of globalization of exchanges, launched at the end of the Cold War.

Notes

1 MOST drug program, UNESCO/UNDCP.
2 On the laundering of the drug money from Hong Kong and Bangkok to Phnom Penh, cf. Sam Rainsy, Cambodian Finance Minister, in *La Dépêche internationale des drogues*, OGD, no. 37, November 1994. On the laundering of the *yakuza*, cf. Interpol, quoted by Radio Australia, 1 May 1997 in SWB BBC Asia-Pacific, 2 May 1997. On the complicities in the Army and at the State summit, cf. Radio Australia, 16 November 1995 in SWB BBC Asia-Pacific, 20 November 1995, as well as the open letter of Sam Rainsy, former Finance Minister in *Sapordarmean Wat Phum*, Phnom Penh, 8 March 1996 in SWB BBC Asia-Pacific, 9 March 1996; *Reaksmei Kampuchea*, 19 September 1995, pp. 1–5, in SWB BBC Asia-Pacific, 20 September 1995. Cf. also research by the *Far Eastern Economic Review*, 'Medellin on the Mekong', 23 November 1995 and *Far Eastern Economic Review*, 30 November 1995.
3 Cf. *La Dépêche internationale des drogues*, OGD, no. 75, January 1998.
4 Cf. Central News Agency, Taibei, 29 December 1996 in SWB BBC Asia-Pacific, 1 January 1997.
5 Cf. *Free China Review*, 29 November 1996; *The Economist*, 30 November 1996.
6 Cf. David Kempf, 'Mains propres à Taïwan: lutte contre la corruption et émergence d'un nouvel enjeu politique', *Perspectives chinoises*, November–December 1996.
7 Cf. James A. Robinson, *The Free China Journal*, 30 October 1997, p. 7.
8 Cf. Thomas Gold, 'Democratic Scorecard', *Free China Review*, November 1995, p. 48.
9 Cf. *The Free China Journal*, 12 October 1996, p. 3.
10 Cf. Pierre Noël Giraud, *L'inégalité du monde*, Editions Gallimard, 1997, the actual Folio Collection.
11 Cf. *World Drug Report*, UNDCP, Oxford University Press, 1997, p. 131. For the American cocaine market, cf. Mathea Falco, 'America's drug problem and its policy of denial', *Current History*, April 1998, p. 149.

12 Cf. Marie Christine Dupuis, *Stupéfiants, prix, profits: l'économie politique du marché des stupéfiants industriels*, PUF, 1996; *World Drug Report*, UNDCP, Oxford University Press, 1997, p. 131.

13 For an illustration of the economic effects of the drug in the Andean countries, who are not limited to the 'Dutch disease', cf. Pierre Salama, 'Macro-économie de la drogue dans les pays andins', *Futuribles* no. 185, March 1994. Cf. also German Fonseca, 'Economie de la drogue: taille, caractéristique et impact économique', *Tiers-Monde*, July–September 1992.

14 Cf. Marie-Christine Dupuis, *Stupéfiants, prix, profits*, PUF, 1997, pp. 133 and 152. Certain estimates are for 800 000–1 million addicts in Burma, two-thirds of whom smoke opium, and one-third heroin: cf. Ronald D. Renard, *The Burmese Connection, Illegal Drugs and the Making of the Golden Triangle*, Boulder, London, 1996, p. 98.

15 Cf. Peter Zirnite, 'The militarisation of the drug war in Latin America', *Current History*, April 1998.

16 Cf. Mathea Falco, 'America's drug problem and its policy of denial', *Current History*, April 1998.

17 Cf. Eva Bertram and Kenneth Sharpe, *World Policy Journal*, Winter 1997, quoted in Peter Zirnite, 'The militarisation of the drug war', p. 172. Our conclusion differs here from that of Peter Zirnite.

18 Cf. Denis Robert, *La justice ou le cahos*, Editions Stock, 1997; Jean de Maillard, *Un monde sans loi: la criminalité financière en images*, Editions Stock, 1998.

19 For a very stimulating analysis of the relationships between crime and globalization, cf. Jean de Maillard, 'Le crime à venir', *Le débat*, March–April 1997.

20 Cf. Samuel Huntington, quoted in Jean Cartier-Bresson, 'Eléments d'analyse pour une économie de la corruption', *Tiers-Monde* revue, July–September 1992.

21 Cf. Jean-François Bayart *et al. La criminalisation de l'Etat en Afrique*, Editions Complexe, 1997.

22 Cf. *Financial Times*, 10 June 1998.

23 Cf. *New York Times*, 3 June 1998, p. 8.

24 Cf. *Business Eastern Europe*, Economist Intelligence Unit, 22 September 1997.

25 Cf. Vito Tanzi, 'Money laundering and the international financial system', IMF Working papers, May 1996; cf. also Peter Quirk, 'Macro-economic implications of money laundering', IMF Working papers, June 1996. These two studies remain very general and do not allude to precise examples.

26 See Chapter 2.

27 See Chapters 2 and 3.

28 Cf. Guilhem Fabre, 'Hong Kong: vers un modèle singapourien?' *Le Monde diplomatique*, May 1997, and 'Hong Kong: la lessiveuse chinoise', *La Dépêche internationale des drogues*, July 1996.

29 Cf. Wang Anpei, 'Zhongguo zujin guimou de dongtaï kaocha' (Dynamics analysis of rent-seeking size in China), *Jingji yanjiu* (Economic research), Peking, no. 2, 1995, pp. 75–80. Cf. also Guilhem Fabre, 'The Chinese mirror of transition', *Communist Economies and Economic Transformations*, vol. 4, no. 2, 1992; 'La nouvelle *nouvelle classe*, Réflexions sur la transition en Chine', *Transitions Review*, Université Libre de Bruxelles, 1994, no. 2.

30 Cf. Xie Jiajin, Director of the real estate department at the Ministry of Construction, *China Daily*, 27 October 1997.

31 Calculation made according to an article in *Liaowang* (Outlook), quoted in *China Daily*, 'Real estate should be under control', 30 January 1996, p. 4.

32 Cf. Yuan Zheng Cao, Gang Fan and Wing Thye Woo, 'Chinese economic reforms: past successes and futures challenges', in *Economies in transition: comparing Asia and Eastern Europe*, edited by Wing Thye Woo, Stephen Parker and Jeffrey Sachs, The MIT Press, Cambridge, Mass. 1997, p. 33.

33 The only study which puts aside their economic impact remains to our knowledge the work of Zhu Delin *et al.*, *Zhongguo huiheisi jingrong, shichang fengyun yu lixing sikao* (The grey and black finances in China, reflections on the market fluctuations and rationalities), Shanghai, Lixin huiji chubanshe, 1997, p. 256.

34 Cf. Agence Xinhua, 6 March 1998, in SWB BBC Asia-Pacific, 11 March 1998.

35 Cf. Ricky Tung, 'The depletion of state assets in mainland China', *Issues and Studies*, Taibei, no. 1, 1996, pp. 3–4.

36 Cf. *China Economic News*, 16 June 1997 and Yuang Zheng Cao, Gang Fan and Wing Thye Woo, 'Chinese economic reforms', p. 34.

37 *China Economic News*, 9 March 1998.

38 Cf. *Financial Times*, 24 June 1997.